Make a Joyful Noise!

A Brief History of Gospel Music

Ministry in America

Kathryn B. Kemp

JOYFUL NOISE PRESS

Make a Joyful Noise! A Brief History of Gospel Music Ministry in America

© 2011 by Kathryn B. Kemp

Published by Joyful Noise Press, Chicago, Illinois

Queries regarding rights and permissions should be addressed to:

Joyful Noise Press, 8708 S. Bennett, PMB 410, Chicago, IL 60617

Manufactured in the United States of America

Publisher's Cataloging-In-Publication Data
(Prepared by The Donohue Group, Inc.)

Kemp, Kathryn B.
  Make a joyful noise! : a brief history of gospel music ministry in America / by Kathryn B. Kemp.

  p. : ill. ; cm.

  "A brief history of the gospel music ministry in America from pre-slavery to the beginning of the 21st century, and the impact of the Gospel Music Workshop of America on the genre."--T.p.
  Includes bibliographical references and index.
  ISBN: 978-0-9833630-0-2

  1. Gospel music--United States--History and criticism. 2. African Americans--Music--History and criticism. 3. Spirituals (Songs)--United States--History. 4. Dorsey, Thomas Andrew--Influence. 5. Cleveland, James--Influence. 6. Gospel Music Workshop of America. Mass Choir--Influence. I. Title.

ML3187 .K46 2011
782.254/09

ISBN: 978-0-9833630-0-2

Dedication

God has directed and ordered my steps since the vision of this book was given to me. All praise, honor and glory belong to Him. This book could not have been written without His guidance, illumination, and revelation.

Table of Contents

About the Author

Kathryn Baker Kemp is a product of the Chicago Public Schools. She holds degrees from De Paul University (BA), Chicago State University (MS Ed), and Northern Illinois University (Ed.D). Her career as an educator encompassed duties as an elementary teacher, elementary counselor, high school dean, middle school assistant principal, and elementary school principal within CPS. She also taught as an adjunct faculty member for Northern Illinois University at the College of Du Page in Du Page County, Illinois.

Dr. Kemp's music ministry began with her first job as pianist for the Junior Choir of the Morning Star Baptist Church in Chicago. It ended in 2009 after 40 years of music ministry as organist, pianist, choir member, assistant choir director, minister of music, and director of music at Memorial M.B. Church in Chicago. Currently, she is active in the teaching ministry of her church. In April 2011, she became a licensed Baptist minister. She has been a member of the Chicago Metropolitan Allegro Mass Chapter of the Gospel Music Workshop of America since 2003 and a member of the national academic faculty of GMWA since 2007.

The author has worked as a volunteer with civic and social groups with an emphasis on the youth and the elderly, who are her passion, and has also served on educational and financial advisory boards. One of her favorite scriptures, which guides her daily, is Psalm 121.

Foreword

Make a Joyful Noise! A Brief History of Gospel Music Ministry in America is a valuable resource for the general reader as well as for gospel music enthusiasts. It gives thorough details and historical highlights of gospel music trends up to the 21st century. This compilation traces the roots of gospel music from its Biblical perspective, the basis of its meaning, and provides information on some of the pioneers of gospel, namely: Thomas A. Dorsey, the "Father of Gospel"; Sallie Martin; Rev. James Cleveland, and many others. It also provides information on gospel music partnerships such as The National Convention of Gospel Choirs and Choruses, along with the Gospel Music Workshop of America, founded by the late Rev. James Cleveland.

Each of the six chapters provides information and research that will enlighten the reader. Highlights of the Gospel Music Workshop of America, as it emerged to be the largest organization of its kind, are cited. Primary source material from some of the individuals who labored to preserve the heritage of gospel music comprises a significant component of "Interviews with Gospel Griots," and is a welcome addition to the book.

Gospel music has come a long way. It is in the mainstream and is being performed in places to which it was previously closed (Catholic masses, prominent cathedrals, schools, colleges and universities). Gospel music transcends all boundaries and nationalities. People can share common bonds through gospel music.

From Africa to the New World, America, our peo-ple sang. Some made it through the Middle Passage, while many did not survive. They were torn from their homeland, their loved ones and culture entering the door of no return. They were put on auction blocks, and toiled without pay. Although slavery was full of pain and grief, a song was born— the Negro Spiritual.

Our ancestors sang songs such as "Steal Away," "Nobody Knows the Trouble I've Seen," and "Sometimes I Feel Like a Motherless Child." Sometimes the hardships seemed to be unbearable, and they thought that the only way out was to die, to cross the "River of Jordan," and go home to be with the Lord.

After the abolition of slavery, a more happy and jubilant music arrived on the scene, and it was gospel music. Today, we cherish this great body of music. It is hoped that a greater awareness of and appreciation for this music will unfold as the reader journeys through the history and contents of this book.

Joan Hillsman, PhD

Music Educator, Collegiate Professor
GMWA National Board Member
Director of Academics and GMWA Faculty
African American Music Research Historian

Acknowledgments

I wish to thank all of the members of GMWA, Inc. who have helped and encouraged me in this endeavor. Special thanks are extended to all who completed interviews and questionnaires to help me refine my topic.

Additionally, I thank Geraldine and James Ford, Dr. Joan Hillsman, Elder W. M. Fuqua, the staff of the GMWA Library, and Dean Charles F. Reese, Academic Division, for their assistance in my research. Thanks are also ex-tended to the following persons and organizations:

- Columbia College Chicago Center for Black Music Research
- Doris Dorsey for the photo of Thomas A. Dorsey
- Stephen Miller for technical support and en-couragement
- Dr. Nathan L. Schaffer, Jr. for his enthusiastic encouragement and support

I would also like to thank my family for their support and encouragement, without which this book couldn't have been written.

Mr. Mark A. Boone, my editor, guide, and developer for the duration of this project is sincerely acknowledged for his rigor, insight, and professionalism. With patience and skill, he has helped me craft an idea into a work of art.

Introduction

Make a Joyful Noise!: A Brief History of Gospel Music Ministry in America is the story of the resiliency of an African American people who found their God—even in the midst of brutal oppression—and made music in praise and thanksgiving. This book shows how music—gospel music in particular—has been a vehicle utilized over the years by people of African ancestry as a means of escape, an expression of joy, and source of peace. This music has helped us to hold onto our hopes and dreams despite slavery, Jim Crow laws, segregation, and racism and to instill in our children hope for a better world both here on earth and in the world to come.

Make a Joyful Noise!: A Brief History of Gospel Music Ministry in America was also written to show how the gifts of the Spirit operate in people for the benefit and uplifting of all. The "Father of Gospel Music" Rev. Thomas A. Dorsey, and the "Crown Prince of Gospel Music," Rev. James Cleveland, were the conduits through which this music was conveyed to the American public and the world. The Gospel Music Workshop of America, Inc., the brainchild of Rev. James Cleveland, has played a key role in this mission for more than 40 years, and the author, who has attended the annual Workshops since 2002, focuses on the organization in Part 2 of this book.

Part 1, *Make a Joyful Noise!: A Brief History of Gospel Music Ministry in America* begins with the biblical history of music in worship to God. Shifting to Africa, it shows how the African people preserved their music, their dignity and their heritage in the face of overwhelming odds while transported as human cargo to the new land of America. It travels through the history of America and its people of color, tracing the power and heritage of music to preserve and uplift the psyche of an oppressed people who fought for equality and freedom, with a song on their lips to praise God each step of the way.

PART ONE

The History of Gospel Music from Pre-Slavery to the Early 21st Century

Gospel as a distinct musical genre has a long rich history that pre-dates our enslaved ancestors' arrival on these shores. It begins with the instruments used in the religious rituals of African tribes as diverse as the Asantes and the Bantus to the songs Africans sang on the transatlantic slave ships en route to the Americas. The gospel music thread extends to the "code songs" that slaves sang to communicate their plans to escape the horrors of slavery in the South.

The spirituals that were the creative offshoot of these code songs, influenced the secular "gospel blues" made famous by the "Father of Gospel Music," Dr. Thomas A. Dorsey. Gospel evolved further with the heir to the Dorsey legacy, Rev. James Cleveland, who, for 30 years contributed more to the acceptance of the genre than any other musician.

James Cleveland mentored a young generation of gospel performers who have ushered the genre into the twenty-first century and to widespread secular acceptance with their rap and hip-hop interpretation of the gospel message. In Chapter 1, the author traces the roots of gospel music ministry from its biblical basis to its African heritage. Chapter 2 discusses gospel music of the early twentieth century under the influence of Professor Thomas A. Dorsey. Chapter 3 follows gospel music to the end of the twentieth century, under the influence of Rev. James Cleveland, and Chapter 4 examines the musical heirs to James Cleveland in contemporary gospel music.

Chapter One:

The Roots of Gospel Music Ministry

"Make a joyful song unto the Lord, all ye lands.
Serve the Lord with gladness: come before his presence
with singing."
—Psalm 100: 1-2

The proper place of gospel music in today's music ministry is often debated. Gospel music, in general, is defined as Christian music that expresses a religious belief. Its primary theme is praise, thanksgiving, and adoration to God the Father, Jesus Christ, and the Holy Spirit. *The Dictionary of Fine Arts* defines gospel as "intense joyful music that is associated with evangelists of the South—especially among African Americans" (Hirsch 2002).

While praise and worship services in Protestant and Pentecostal churches feature gospel music to prepare the hearts of the faithful for the message of God's Word, gospel music is also a fine art, as acknowledged in *The Dictionary of Fine Arts*. It is sung, played, and performed in many venues beyond the church setting. *The Columbia Encyclopedia* classifies gospel music as "...the American folk music ... of enslaved African Americans from West Africa, converted to Christianity in the South" (2011). *The Oxford Grove Music Encyclopedia* describes it as "the shared religious heritage of both blacks and evangelical whites" (1994).

Gospel music has its own distinctive style. It is repetitive in nature and allows the audience to join in the experience through what is known as "call and response." The leader calls a word or phrase, and the choir and audience answer in response. Gospel music draws primarily on two black musical traditions: the spirituals and lined hymns of the 1700s through the 1900s and the blues and jazz rhythms of the twentieth century. Blues and jazz rhythms, known for their syncopated beat, are sung *behind* or *after* the beat—a marked distinction from hymns and anthems. The singing of gospel music is accompanied by a variety of instruments and is punctuated by the hands and feet of the singers and audience.

Jazz and gospel music share similarities in composition, both in their note structures and rhythms. The music appeals directly to the emotions of the listeners, who pat their feet and beat or clap their hands in accompaniment to both musical styles. Critics, for this reason, argue that the only difference between the two forms is where they are played: one in secular venues and the other in religious services. This distinction has been blurred since the latter part of the twentieth century, however, as both musical genres are performed on stages, in auditoriums, and in concert halls, with gospel music no longer restricted to religious services. The human voice, piano, organ, harmonica, guitars (lead and bass), steel drums, saxophone, and horn are frequently used in all of these musical genres.

The Biblical Basis for Gospel Music

Gospel music as a ministry derives its heritage from the Bible. *Strong's Lexicon* defines the Hebrew 'sharith' from the Old Testament and the Greek 'diakonia' from the New Testament as terms that relate ministry to spiritual or religious service. Moreover, it views music ministry as both an office and as work, referring to it as the service of believers (Vine 2009). The Greek "leitourgia" from which the word *liturgy* is derived also describes ministry as an office or duty.

Music didn't originate with the Hebrews, but they were the first to integrate it into the worship of Jehovah. The Egyptians and Greek civilizations also wove music into their culture and religious ceremonies. References to the importance and practice of "musick" abound in Old Testament literature. The term *musick* described praise with instruments in the Old Testament accompanied with singing, dancing, and joy. We first learn of Jubal in Genesis 4:21: the "father of all such as handle the harp and organ." *Easton's Bible Dictionary* defines harp and organ as being synonymous with the harp and flute, lyre, and pipe (2009). Musical instruments found in Old Testament scriptures include the cornet, flute, harp, sackbut, tambourines, psaltery, dulcimer, human voice, trumpets, cymbals, triangles, timbrel, and drums. The concept of praise was present in the Hebrew language long before the Psalms were composed (Noble 1986). Judah was the fourth son of Jacob and Leah. His name Judah, "Yehudah"... means praise (23).

The "golden period of poetry and music" in the Hebrew culture began in the period of Samuel and expanded with David and Solomon. Music was a part of all priestly training, and musicians were associated with the spirit of prophesy and of service.

Osbeck states that there are approximately 13 different instruments which could be classified as string instruments, wind instruments, or instruments of percussion, and he has documented the references to music in 44 of the 66 books in the Old and New Testament of the Bible (Osbeck 1998, 18).

Trained professional singers are also present in music ministry from the Old Testament. The temple was a great school of music that trained singers and players of instruments used for conducting services. A class of professional singers was employed for temple worship. Musical training was also important in private Hebrew life. Children were instructed in vocal and instrumental music (Easton 2009).

Psalms as Music. Psalms were written for the musical selections performed by members of the Levitical families who were in charge of temple worship services (Numbers 8:14-16). The Book of Psalms was used for all phases of temple worship. King David, greatly beloved by God, wrote many psalms for the chief musicians who played stringed instruments. He composed many songs with specific musicians in mind. The sons of Korah, chief musicians in the temple, received the legacy of the majority of David's temple worship songs. Asaph was credited for writing psalms as well. Specific psalms were written for individual musicians who were identified by name or location, in addition to the sons of Korah. Psalms were written as songs, prayers, dedications, remembrances, meditations, praise, penitence, expressions of mourning, and for special people and specific occasions.

Music Ministry in the New Testament. The New Testament church also incorporated music ministry in its worship services. The persecution of Christians by the Romans and some Jewish clergy made house meetings the most common form of communal worship. Songs and prayer were a part of these church services. Christians were urged to speak to each other "with psalms and hymns and spiritual songs, singing, and making melody in your heart to the Lord" (Ephesians 5:19). The last chapter of the New Testament, Revelation, speaks of the ministry of worship in praise and song to the "Lamb of God."

The tradition of music in worship continued with the advent of Christianity—ushered in by Constantine the Great. He made Christianity the official religion in A.D.313. The clergy led the liturgical service, although the individual worshipper was encouraged to participate in congregational singing. The liturgy of the Mass was established during the era known as the Dark Ages. Gregorian chants were introduced by St. Gregory the Great during the sixth century. The growth of harmony occurred during this thousand-year period (Osbeck 20-21).

Music and the Reformation

Martin Luther did much to bring about joy in religious worship akin to that seen in the early apostolic church. With the Reformation, Christians again found joy in worship. Congregational singing received greater attention by religious reformers such as John Calvin and Ulrich Zwingli. The Reformation was experienced differently in the different European countries. King Henry VIII established the Church of England in 1534. The Anglican Church, also known as the Church of England, 15 years later in 1549, published the *Book of Common Prayer* which formalized the rituals of the Church's worship services–distinctive from that of the Roman Catholic Church.

The Puritans didn't agree fully with the Anglican Church, but during the reign of Queen Elizabeth were unable to effect change within the church. The ascension to the throne of James I (1603-1625) and Charles I (1625-1649) brought a more favorable climate for the Puritans. Tensions continued between the established Roman Catholic Church and the Anglican Church. Puritans followed the reformist teachings of John Calvin by accepting the authority of the Scriptures and adopting the psalms for congregational singing. However, some fanatical Puritans who didn't believe in choirs or church organs destroyed churches in England during those tumultuous times.

The Anglican Church liturgy was re-established when Charles II (1660-1685) assumed the throne of England. The anthem was developed during this time. Tensions continued between the established church and minority groups during the 17th century. A change came in the 18th century with Isaac Watts, often called the "father of English hymnody." This ultimately would be the musical tradition that enslaved African Americans were introduced to in the churches of the Colonial South (Osbeck 22-24)

Isaac Watts (1674-1748) was a precocious child born prematurely. His parents were non-Anglican dissenters. Isaac learned Latin at four, Greek at nine, and Hebrew at age 13. He was challenged by his father Isaac Sr. to write his own hymn after the young Isaac expressed dissatisfaction with the authorized church versions. Isaac Watts went on to write more than 700 hymns which are still sung more than 300 years after his death. One of his most famous hymns is "Alas and Did My Savior Bleed" (Morgan 2003, 31-33). Watts' arrangement of "Joy to the World" is a standard well-known and loved Christmas hymn.

The Advent of Gospel Music

The word *gospel* is variously defined as "God's spell," "good spell," or "good news." It comes from the Greek word *evangelio*, translated as "good message" (Easton 2009). The Book of Acts (20:24) refers to: "the gospel of the grace of God," and Ephesians to the "gospel of salvation." *The International Standard Bible Dictionary* (2009) defines the word gospel as the Anglo-Saxon derivation of "the story concerning God," stating further that it is known entirely by revelation and not law because laws are commands based on works, while gospel is salvation based on grace.

Gospel Music Defined. All over the world gospel music is defined by *American Heritage Dictionary* as "a kind of Christian music based on American folk music, marked by strong rhythms and elaborated refrains, and incorporating elements of spirituals, blues, and jazz" (2009). Its history begins with the experiences of enslaved African-American people who adapted the religion of their oppressors, translating the message of God's love into a religion that had meaning for their unique circumstances. This message was first communicated in song. These songs became the origin of American folk music and the genesis of all American musical genres that followed.

Banfield (2010) speaks of music and cultural codes. He has devised a philosophy of music that explains how music is coded by one's ancestry and experiences.

> Black musicians from every corner of the world, speak from a "Black culturalistic view"....We have to provide a human and cultural dimension to learn the music fully....Humans are a product of culture and a larger creative universe-God, spirit, creativity....One theological/analysis lens through which we can see this is the transfer of West African codes of griot musicians who used music as the "framework" through which all life was mediated....This was first heard in the slave hollers, work songs, and spirituals (53-55).

The Message of Gospel Music. The message of gospel music is salvation. The music inspires hope and faith in the future, drawing from the "grace gifts" of God shared by Paul in 1 Corinthians, Chapters 12-14. These spiritual gifts are referenced again in Ephesians 4, Romans 12, and 1 Peter 5:10. The message is clear to all who see, hear, and believe: We, as followers of Christ, as his disciples, as stewards of the gifts of grace that we have received from God, are responsible for doing the work of Him who sent us. Thus, Christians involved in the gospel music ministry, are charged with the duty to share the message of the gospel, to offer opportunities for salvation, to edify the body of Christ, and to increase membership in the body of Christ—the Church. Servants in gospel music ministry are called to evangelize through their music. Their primary objective is to glorify God and to offer God's salvation to sinners.

Music and Worship

Music is the dominant accompaniment to the worship experience in contemporary corporate church settings. Nearly all organized religions provide books, hymnals, or electronic means of communicating to the worshipper the songs that will be an integral part of the worship service. Instruments and voices swell in songs of praise and worship to our God. The foreword to the well known book *Celebration Hymnal: Songs and Hymns for Worship* attests to the importance of song in worship in the following ways:

- Song is personified as "the climate in which God Himself works in His most glorious way as Creator (Job 38:4-7).
- Song is the companion means by which we are taught to see the Word of God enriched in its workings within our lives in practice and purity (Colossians 3:16-17).
- Song is the conduit by which the souls' night of darkness is ignited with hope

and deliverance (Job 35:10; Psalm 32:6-7.)
- Song is the claim of the barren, by which God says we may entertain and expect fruitfulness (Isaiah 54:1).
- Song is the conquering instrument available when we are outnumbered by circumstances (2 Chronicles 20:21-22)."

The foreword ends by sharing the significance of song to our spiritual lives: "The secret of song is the church's most distinctive resource, not because music is more powerful than the Word or the Spirit, but because song is a means by which both can become so joyously conjoined – by ALL the people of the Lord!" (1977).

The publisher's note in the *Baptist Hymnal* 1883 gives this explanation for the hymnal: "The Publication Society trusts that this book will be acceptable in churches in all parts of the country and a real addition to the Service of Praise (Publisher's Note, B. Griffin—Secretary)."

Praise and Worship in Church Settings. In his book *Perspectives of Praise and Worship* (1997), Dr. Robert Mitchell Simmons, former Dean of the Academic Faculty of the Gospel Music Workshop of America (GMWA), also speaks to the role of praise and worship in church settings. Dr. Simmons says:

> Praise and worship isn't new. It existed in the devotional services of deacons; in the Pentecostal meetings, and in contemporary praise and worship with keyboard, percussion, and song leaders. [Moreover], the traditional concept of "devotions" carried

the purpose of "getting ready for worship." This devotion was done to prepare the congregation spiritually and emotionally in anticipation of the worship liturgy yet to come (6-7).

Simmons continues by differentiating how this experience is viewed in churches:

Praise and worship for some is an entire worship experience that has energy, vitality, and excitement. To others, praise and worship is a song and testimony service that is a prelude to worship's liturgy. This latter perspective of praise and worship is one that seeks to bring the worshipers into the worship experience with a feeling of energy, vitality, and excitement--a sense of high anticipation (7).

The church members, however, are those who provide the "energy of the worship service." Energies, visions and creativity within the congregation are used in the "energized worship." As the journey from the personal confines of individual members to a just and cohesive community of God takes place, the "energized worship" response asks individuals to envision themselves in roles of liturgical leadership and congregational responsiveness. The knowledge base of the person affects the experiencing of this energy. (12-13).

Gospel Music within the Church Setting.
In the church setting gospel music comple-
ments and supports the service, particularly at services that preach evangelism. The
minister of music is responsible for selecting
songs that present the Word of God, His plan
for Salvation, and convey the essence of spiritual renewal. Dr. Simmons, in *Evangelism in
Gospel Music* (1976), posits that the lyrics in
black music ministry fall within four basic
categories:

* the nature and character of God and Jesus Christ
* the nature of man
* the relationship between God and man
* the Holy Scriptures as the Word of God
  (15).

Simmons stresses that the importance of musical interpretation is both in the lyrics and in the
delivery. This is conveyed through the lyrics, the
music director, and the instrumentalists (24).
***Gospel Music and the Mainstream Black
Church.*** Gospel music was not fully accepted
in mainstream black churches until the mid-
1930s. It disapproved of the rhythm, synco-
pation, and resemblance to blues and jazz
traditions. Much of this rejection was based
on the need of churches in the North to distance themselves from the struggles, pov-
erty, and religion of blacks newly migrated
to the eastern, midwestern, and western cities. Music viewed as "southern" and "country" found no home in these places. Worship
services in these churches featured anthems

and "dignified" spirituals, which were sung along with the traditional hymns brought to the United States by the Episcopalians—the American members of the Anglican Church.

African Religious Traditions

The religion of African peoples was much different in Africa than on the new American continent. Ancestor worship was common, and polytheism—the worship of many gods—was pervasive. African peoples observed many rituals and designated participants carried out prescribed duties based on the particular African rite. They fashioned instruments to be used in religious ceremonies and for special occasions. These ceremonies varied among the different tribes—from Yoruba priestesses, to the Wolof States, the Oyo, the Asante Empire, Dahomeans, Bini, Akan-Ashanti, and the Bantu-speaking Lala tribe—all of which found their way into the music of enslaved African peoples in America and in the music they gave to their new homeland and ultimately back to the world (Darden 2004).

Through forced slavery, the various religious styles of worship were transferred to the North American continent. Musical traditions from Africa are found throughout Latin America, the Caribbean Islands, and the United States. Conferences on ethnomusicology are held at well-known colleges and universities throughout the United States and in Europe. The focus of the research is to study and appreciate the import and value of African music traditions to all forms of music that exist today throughout the world.

Researchers point to the influence of African Americans on music beginning before the first arrival of Africans to Virginia in 1629. Historians use logs of transatlantic slave ships to document the use of music by the captives. The captains allowed the slaves to sing in an effort to keep the captives in the best physical and mental state possible for their eventual sale on the auction blocks. W.E.B. DuBois (1903, 117) wrote that the best part of America came from Negro slave music:

> Negro folk song – the rhythmic cry of the slave – stands today not simply as the sole American music, but as the most beautiful expression of human experience born this side of the seas. It has been neglected, it has been, and is, half-despised, and above all it has been persistently mistaken and misunderstood: but notwithstanding, it still remains as the singular spiritual heritage of the nation and the greatest gift of the Negro people.

Slave Worship Traditions

The ring shout was an African tradition incorporated into slave worship traditions in the southern United States. It embodied the sacred religious rituals of African dance, which was devotional, sometimes spontaneous, and had elements of prayer, usually directed toward their religious gods. Nearly 10 million Songhai, Ibo, Yoruba, and Akans left the mother continent of Africa for the horrors of the Middle Passage to become slaves on plantations in America and the Caribbean Islands. Unlike the Hebrews who could not sing in a strange land, the African enslaved population forged a new song and melody from the music of the masters and created meaningful music—with new melodies, which became spirituals, gospel hymns, and then gospel music–music that had never been heard, and that never existed before blacks came to this continent.

These black hymns would be sung at church services and at traditional events in black community life: weddings, funerals, baptisms, and church socials. They are included in the collection *Slave Songs of the United States*, published originally in 1867. Said the editors, William Francis Allen, Charles Pickard Ware, and Lucy McCoy Garrison in the introduction:

> It is difficult to express the entire character of these Negro ballads by mere musical notes and signs. The odd turns made in the throat and the curious rhythmic effect produced by single voices chiming in at different irregular intervals seem almost as impossible to place on the score as the singing of birds or the tones of an Aeolian harp (54-55).

Worship in a Strange Land. Slaves in the Colonial South attended the same church as the slave owners. They were separated from the whites but allowed to sit either in the back of the church or the balcony. They learned the hymns of the Anglican Church from these experiences. Hymnody in African American churches was therefore based in a large part on the tradition of European hymns slaves learned in the church services of their masters.

Slave owners eventually realized that the enslaved blacks communicated in code through song, which led to the slaves' participation in uprisings and revolts. Whites in the northern states refused to allow blacks to worship separately because of these slave revolts and uprisings. This ban on separate church services for blacks and whites continued throughout the colonial period in America.

"Bush Harbor Devotions." The term "bush harbor" or "hush arbor" are terms that described the separate religious devotions of blacks during slavery. Blacks would go to secret places to conduct worship services where they felt free to express their emotions hidden from the masters that oppressed them. There was no need for a formal preacher at these services. A person—the caller—sung, and the group responded.

These devotional prayer meetings were marked by clapping, shouting, feet stomping, rocking, and shouting. People were stationed along the paths to these secret meetings to signal the slaves if any whites were approaching. The meeting places were hidden and camouflaged. Blacks, at these meetings, sung spirituals that expressed how they felt about their harsh treatment in the country they now called home.

The spiritual and "call and response" became a part of the Sunday worship experience of blacks in the rural black southern churches organized after the Civil War. Outpourings of emotions and release in song were manifested in the devotions, prayer meetings, weekly Bible classes, camp meetings and revivals within the black church. Members accepted salvation through an emotional personal connection and response to the message of these songs that had become sacred to the black rural church. This experience was a sign of salvation, of "getting the Holy Ghost."

The emotion displayed at those services was thought of as a form of "possession" by more refined African Americans from the North, whose worship services mirrored the mainstream Anglicized form of worship. They viewed their use and adaptation of the European classical style as a way, through assimilation, to gain access to the white society to which they had been denied during slavery. The worship music in these churches was sung without the enthusiasm and gestures common to the rural black church. Blacks who had migrated from the South to the North after World War I missed the richness of the worship services they had left behind.

Hymns of the Early African American Church
The African Methodist Episcopal Church was the first independent denomination formed by post-Emancipation blacks. A group of blacks who had held separate organized prayer meetings while simultaneously attending a white church in Philadelphia came together in November 1878 under the leadership of Bishop Richard Allen to form Bethel A.M.E. Church. Allen duplicated the liturgical order of the white church to prove to whites that blacks could be assimilated into American society as equals. The music composed by blacks of that time mimicked the existing music of hymns and psalms sung in the Methodist

and Anglican churches. Allen published this music in the *Collection of Spiritual Songs.*

Although it was not difficult for African Americans to adapt their spiritual beliefs to the Christian faith of the oppressor, their African roots remained intact in the music adopted from the white churches. This music spoke eloquently to the conditions experienced in slavery. The storytelling African oral tradition of the griot was preserved in Negro spirituals.

The Dr. Watts Hymns. It was through the Anglican Church of their masters, that Blacks were introduced to the hymns of Englishman Isaac Watts. The "lined hymn," also referred to in the Baptist church as the "Dr. Watts hymn," was the most common hymn sung in these southern worship services. African Americans adapted the hymns to speak to the bondage they experienced from their slave masters. They understood the similarity of the black experience in America to that of the Hebrew people in Egypt during periods of captivity and struggle.

The influence of Isaac Watts is still felt in the music sung in churches today. Watts, dissatisfied with the singing in English churches, began composing hymns at age 20 (Harris 1992). His career made him famous. His hymns became a staple of black worship services and are reported to be responsible for the conversion of many people, including a later famous hymnist, Fanny Crosby (Morgan 2003, 33). Baptist deacons infused these "Dr. Watts" songs with the flavor of the African American culture as they sung them a cappella in morning and mid-week prayer and worship services.

Early Black Hymnists. Evidence exists that
Blacks began composing music and putting
songs together for hymnals as early as the 17th
century. *The Bay Psalm Book* emerged in 1651. It
was a collection of colonial hymns, work songs,
and field hollers (Banfield 88). John Lea, a former slave born in Africa, published a hymnal
with his and others' work entitled a *Collection
of Hymns* (Roach 1992, 97).

Horace Clarence Boyer writes that gospel
music got its start in New England in 1734 with
the evangelistic campaigns of Rev. Jonathan
Edwards (1986). Edwards found that upbeat
hymns with different meter and rhythm were
appreciated in his revival settings. This religious period, known historically as the "Great
Awakening" moved from the eastern to the
southern states. The Free African Society of
1787 was the movement credited with start-
ing independent black worship services in the
East. These services were held as prayer and
devotional meetings independently of the formal white services.

Dr. Charles A. Tindley (1857-1933) is acknowledged as the father of the gospel hymn.
Dr. Tindley, a Methodist preacher, was influenced greatly by the Pentecostal Movement.
His compositions spoke to the experience of
blacks in America. His hymns departed from
the Methodist standard, employed "blues ca-
dences and modified blues stanza long before
blues became popular (Harris 1992, 129)."
Tindley freely encouraged musicians to impro-
vise when playing the compositions he wrote.

Tindley's first congregation was based
in Berlin, Maryland, where his hymns were

first sung. He organized the Tindley Temple United Methodist Church in Philadelphia, and it became one of the largest churches of its time. Tindley's best known compositions are "The Storm is Passing Over," "We'll Understand It Better By and By," and "I'll Overcome Someday." The latter song, popularly known as "We Shall Overcome Some Day," became a mainstay of the Civil Rights Movement of the 1950s and 1960s. There is still debate over whether he should be credited with the arrangement of the civil rights anthem.

Henry "Harry Thacker" Burleigh (1866-1949) was another African American composer and performer of gospel music. Burleigh, a classically trained musician, took spirituals to the concert stage. He attended the National Conservatory of Music in New York City, and travelled throughout the United States and Europe after his graduation from the conservatory. He was a concert artist, arranger, singer, and composer. Burleigh is credited with composing more than 100 songs during his musical career (Darden 2004).

When well-known Czech composer Antonin Dvorak came to the United States in 1892 to assume charge of the National Conservatory in New York, he became intrigued by the plantation songs of his student, Harry Burleigh, who had learned the songs from his grandfather. Dvorak incorporated elements of what he termed "the Negro melodies" into his music—most notably his celebrated "New World Symphony." Dvorak and Burleigh developed a friendship – a relationship that was very controversial at that time.

Dvorak made the following comment in the *New York Herald* after his exposure to Black music during his tenure at the conservatory:

> In the Negro melodies of America I discover all that is needed for a great and noble school of music. They are pathetic, tender, passionate, melancholy, solemn, religious, bold, merry, gay, gracious, whatever you will....There is nothing in the whole range of composition that cannot find thematic source here. I am now satisfied...that the future music of this country must be founded upon what are called the Negro melodies (Williams 2009, 18).

Harry Burleigh is recognized for his solo arrangements of classic spirituals–especially "Deep River" and "Nobody Knows the Trouble I've Seen." His compositions have been performed by choral groups, yet his style of arrangements also permitted great vocalists such as Marian Anderson to perform his work. Anderson was the first black artist to sing at Carnegie Hall. She sung all types of music. Appreciation for gospel music was greatly enhanced by the performances of these early pioneers who spread the "Negro melodies" to a wider audience through concert performances.

The Negro Spiritual

The Negro spiritual—a song that embodied a secret code of hope and freedom from slavery was a creative response to the slaves' oppression in the American South. These songs were sung to signal slaves about planned escapes to Canada, whose code name was

Canaan. Slaves also substituted the word "heaven" with "yonder," the code name for the North, in the song "Going up Yonder." The celebrated conductor of the Underground Railroad, Harriet Tubman was given the code name "Moses." The slaves knew that the spiritual "Go Down, Moses" meant an imminent trip North to the "Promised Land," usually accompanied by the singing of the spiritual "Swing Low, Sweet Chariot."

Spirituals such as "Nobody Knows the Trouble I've Seen" were testimonies of the cruel treatment, sales of children, rape, and beatings that were daily occurrences of life in slavery. Bernice Johnson Reagon speaks eloquently of the narratives of spirituals—what she terms tales of woe: They were tones, loud, long, and deep; breathing the prayer and complaints of souls boiling over with the bitterest anguish. Every tone was a testimony against slavery and a prayer to God for deliverance from chains (2001, 73). Reagon explains further:

> Negro spirituals were acknowledged as a sacred art form by some in the southern states: The Negro Spirituals are a distinctly American contribution to the sacred music of the world. They are the spontaneous, unstudied expression of the joys and sorrows of the race as related to religious experience. They were born in the hearts of an uneducated people who could not read or write....But they brought with them a native sense of rhythm and out of their limitations and the varied conditions of kindness and cruelty have

come these melodies and harmonies the like of which are not found in any other part of the world (Rodeheaver 1936, 17).

Some of the spirituals expressed directly the cruelty of the 'massas' and spoke of freeing the slaves. In the preface to the Book of *American Negro Spirituals* for which he was editor, James Weldon Johnson (1925) had much to say regarding the origin of the Negro spiritual:

> It would have been a notable achievement if the white people who settled this country, having a common language and heritage...had created a body of folk music comparable to the Negro Spirituals. But from whom did these songs spring – these songs unsurpassed among the folk songs of the world and in the poignancy of their beauty, unequaled (Rodeheaver 1925, 12)?

The Nashville Singers, best known as the Fisk Jubilee Singers, were the primary ambassadors of spiritual singing to the world after the Reconstruction period in America. Schools were organized throughout the South by white men for "colored people" to obtain a decent education. The school's benefactor, General Clinton B. Fisk, hired George L. White to be the school's treasurer, music professor, and choirmaster.

In 1870, White formed a group of 11 students from Nashville and neighboring towns, to perform classical music at concerts. The group sang a Negro spiritual to close each concert. The Negro spiritual became popular and well received as a result of this exposure. The Nashville Singers were recruited to tour to help raise money when the school experienced severe financial difficulty. The singers enjoyed phenomenal success.

Henry Ward Beecher, the brother of Harriet Beecher Stowe, author of the anti-slavery classic *Uncle Tom's Cabin*, was instrumental in securing a concert engagement for the singers in New York City. This marked the beginning of a full-blown career in which they performed before President Ulysses Grant at the White House, around the United States and in Europe.

The Fisk Jubilee Singers caused racism to rear its ugly head in their concert tours in the United States. They were often refused lodging. They were much surprised and pleased by their reception in Europe. The Duke and Duchess of Argyll heard them sing in London. They arranged a concert for them at their lodge. The Queen of England came at the invitation of the Duke and Duchess. She heard the Jubilee Singers in a private concert. This greatly encouraged the singers, and from this engagement they received distinguished attention throughout their stay. The Prince and Princess of Wales and Prime Minister Gladstone were among other dignitaries who aided the singers in their financial quest for their school.

They also performed in Scotland where they met and sung with Evangelists Moody and Sankey in Newcastle-on-Tyne. They returned to the United States as a huge success with funds to build Jubilee Hall. The structure was completed in 1875. The success of these tours placed additional strains on the budget of the university and its supporters. The Jubilee Singers continued to perform in Europe to raise money for their university (Marsh 1878, 17-99).

The Fisk Jubilee Singers raised more than $170,000 from these engagements, part of which was used to build Jubilee Hall. The site was awarded National Historical Landmark status in 1974. It was the first permanent building as part of Fisk University that was built for the education of black students in the United States. The choral singing first popularized by the Fisk Jubilee Singers became the forerunner of ensembles, glee clubs, quartets, college choruses, and college choirs.

It is important to remember that the Fisk Jubilee Singers were the first generation to be freed by the abolition of slavery in the United States. Their history is unique. Their charge (and burden) was to represent the Negro race with pride and dignity while at the same time being the objects of derision and hatred from many in America. Each member was a professed Christian. As many as 24 persons—during different time periods—formed the Jubilee Singers. Members of the company during the late nineteenth century were: Ella Sheppard, Nashville, Tennessee; Maggie L. Porter, Lebanon, Texas; Jennie Jackson, Nashville, Tennessee; Georgia Gordon, Nashville, Tennessee; Thomas Rutling, Wilson County, Tennessee; Frederick J. Loudin, Portage County, Ohio; Mabel Louis, New Orleans, Louisiana; Minnie Tate, Nashville, Tennessee; Benjamin M. Holmes,

Charleston, South Carolina; and Isaac P. Dickerson, Wytheville, Virginia. (Marsh 1878, 102-119).

The Pentecostal Movement

The Pentecostal Movement occurred after the Civil War Era. It was part of the Holiness Movement that began at a white revival meeting in 1867. The message of the Holiness movement was the "sanctification of the individual through the word of God. Pentecostalism stressed the role of baptism for adults (second birth), and a filling with grace (Blue and Naden 2001, 57)." One manifestation of the spirit is observed in the speaking in tongues, also one of the 'grace gifts' of the Holy Spirit.

Revivals, camp meetings and fiery evangelists preached the gospel to crowds in the North and South. Musician Ira D. Sankey, director of the revival campaigns of evangelist Dwight L. Moody, claims to have heard the phrase "to sing the gospel" in Sunderland, England, in 1873 (59)." Gospel hymns were sung during these evangelistic services. The hymns invited the listener to relate to the gospel message both through song and the preached word. One of the best known rural campfire songs, "A Great Camp Meeting," is a spiritual that might have been sung at one of those large outdoor gatherings where traveling evangelists preached and sang the gospel.

Sister Rosetta Tharpe was a well-known Pentecostal singer who sang both sacred and secular music. She is widely recognized as "a crossover pioneer." She toured with a secular band in 1940, yet sung gospel at the Apollo in 1944. The press compared her to Mahalia Jackson, who sang only gospel, and Jackson eclipsed Tharpe in popularity for that reason.

Tharpe sung abroad during the 1950s. She returned to the United States with the success of her European tours behind her. She died in 1972 after her last public performance at New York's Lincoln Center in 1972 with the gospel singer and pianist Marion Williams. Rosetta Tharpe was a very gifted guitarist. Barney Parks, formerly of the Dixie Hummingbirds recalls that "people would almost break in" to hear her play. Alfred Miller, a Brooklyn church music director attested to her skill in music: "she could do runs, she could do sequences, she could do arpeggios....I mean she could put that guitar behind her and play it (*American Legacy* Summer 2009, 65-66)."

Pentecostal worship was not welcome in some of the 'genteel' black churches; thus, the worshippers who left the Methodist and Baptist churches began a new religious movement. A Baptist minister, Charles H. Mason in 1897 created the Church of God in Christ denomination.

Black Gospel Music under Attack

Black gospel music was not without its detractors. Scholars argued that Black songs were merely White songs with a few changes. Blacks were denied the originality of a new genre of music that began with the spirituals. Reagon also wrestled with the debate over the authenticity of spirituals as black music. Scholars such as George Pullen Jackson of Vanderbilt University in 1933 compared the tunes and texts of Black and White songs from all camp meetings. His conclusion was that all of these songs belonged to White sacred music tradition (Reagon 2001, 77). Noted musicologist and scholar Berniece Reagon researched this controversy:

> At first I pondered over this debate about what was first – were our Sacred songs original? Why was it important? Working out our survival in this land resulted in Black people taking on many aspects of the culture in which we found ourselves. It was the cost of survival. But I was raised to understand that it was not a one-way street, that often the foundation of what has been created in this land came from our culture, our knowledge, and our talents. Why was it important to suggest that our spirituals were revisions of White songs and should not be considered original compositions? As I continued to study American culture, I began to understand the relationship between possession, ownership, and status... If there is any question about knowledge being culturally bound, this discussion is an excellent example... For these scholars, the originality of a genre of new sacred songs created by slaves was unthinkable; so they created analytical models that would demonstrate aspects of the spirituals that were shared with White sacred songs. And with some shared texts, and some shared fragments of melody; the spiri-

tuals were declared reworked White sacred songs! (77-78).

The debate raged through the 1970s. African music (from the continent), southern White music and the spirituals themselves were the genres in question. The conclusion of the experts and studies recognize "the result is a new kind of music, certainly not mere imitation, but more creative and original than any other American music (79)." This was further elaborated on by the words of music historian Eileen Southern who described the phenomenon of the camp meeting in terms of Black music:

> They were singing songs of their own composing, which was even worse in the eyes of the officials. The texts of the composed songs were not lyric poems, the hallowed tradition of Watts, but a stringing together of isolated lines from prayers, the scriptures, and orthodox hymns with the addition of choruses and refrains between the verses...Nevertheless, from such practices emerged a new kind of religious song that became the distinctive badge of the camp meeting movements (79)."

African American Music and American Culture

The significance of African American music to America and the world derives from the ability of people of color to view the world multidimensionally. The ability of Blacks in America to view music from subjective and objective frames of reference helped them perform in self-derisive musical entertainment. The legacy of the slave trade songs was used for profit by whites in vaudeville and minstrel shows after the end of the Civil War in which Black life was mocked by whites during Reconstruction and the Jim Crow eras. Black music, complete with tambourines, song, dancer, and musical instruments, was the mainstay of these performances. The term used by whites for black music written by whites was "Ethiopian" songs. "Camp Town Races," "Old Black Joe,' "Massa's in de Cold, Cold Ground," and "My Old Kentucky Home" are examples of the songs written for the minstrel shows (Harris 1992).

Other musical genres followed that trace their origins to black folk music. Ragtime, barrelhouse blues, blues, and jazz were all precursors to what became referred to as "gospel music." Professor Thomas A. Dorsey, the "Father of Gospel Music," is credited with elevating blues tunes into gospel music, a music he called "gospel blues."

Gospel music continued to be sung, shared and published. Dr. Tindley's hymns were among others published in *The Gospel Pearls*, in 1921 by the National Baptist Convention. Lucie E. Campbell, the choral coordinator for the National Baptist Convention, was instrumental in the publication of the collection of hymns which brought these songs into mainline churches across the country. She was also a noted composer.

"Professor" Evangelist Willie M. Nix also published hymns with elements of blues that became popular songs sung in the black churches. William B. McClain in *Songs of*

Zion (1981) attributes the gospel song to the North. It was the counterpart of the Negro spiritual of the South, finding expression in the larger northern cities of Chicago, New York, and Detroit (x). He compared them to songs of Zion sung in a strange land that told of their struggles and hardships. This translated into praise from their mouths – an expression of their faith:

> The gospel song expresses theology. Not the theology of the academy or the university...but a theology of experience – the theology of a God who sends the sunshine and the rain, the theology of a God who is very much alive and active and who has not forsaken those who are poor and oppressed and unemployed....It is a theology of survival that allows a people to celebrate the ability to continue the journey in spite of the insidious tentacles of racism and oppression and to sing,"It's another day's journey and I'm glad about it (x)."

The use of song to express our story continued to be heard in lyrics. A greater number of blacks began copying the choral style of singing popularized by the Fisk Jubilee Singers in religious services. Dr. James H. Cone speaks of the purpose of religion for blacks in America and the authenticity of our religious practices:

> The blacks brought their religion with them. After a time they accepted the

white man's religion, but they have not always expressed it in the white man's way. It became the black man's purpose perhaps it was his destiny— to shape, to fashion, to re-create the religion offered him by the Christian slave master, to remold it nearer to his own heart's desire, nearer to his own peculiar needs. The black religious experience is something more than a black patina on a white happening. It is a unique response to an historical occurrence which can never be replicated for any people in America (1970, 8).

The heritage of gospel music has been traced from its historical, scriptural, musical, and cultural roots. It has evolved into a uniquely American genre that inspired a people, and became infused with the pain and joy that they expressed through their music.

Gospel music, as an art form, gained strength through corporate worship in its mission to evangelize and to uplift. This music was initially opposed by many within the emerging black church. The opposition to gospel music was eventually overcome. The gospel choir, therefore, became a fixture in the African American worship experience. Today, gospel music is firmly established and rooted in the African American spiritual and cultural tradition.

Chapter Two:

Gospel Music of the Early Twentieth Century

"Precious Lord, Take my hand. Lead me on, help me stand.
I am tired, I am weak, I am worn...."
—Thomas A. Dorsey

By the 1920s, spirituals were firmly established in the worship experience of
AME churches. The "new spiritual"
was sung along with the western European
anthem in morning services and monthly
musicals. Members and choirs alike were
able to express their emotions in a manner
similar to that of the bush harbor meetings,
which provided a shared sense of unity in a
dignified manner based on a common historical experience. The spiritual in this form
became an accepted part of the institutional
urban old-line church.

Protestant pastors in the 1920s and1930s
faced a dilemma, however. Would they ig-
nore the appeal that gospel blues had to their
congregations? Moreover, how could they
keep the sanctity of the more formal Anglican Church worship service and still meet
the needs of the blacks who felt disenfran-
chised by the white majority? The pastors
recognized the inability of the present worship service of assimilation to lift the spir-
its of the members and give them the same
sense of purpose and fulfillment that they

enjoyed from the spirited interaction and communal unity of the bush harbor meeting. How could they keep their members from leaving what they considered lifeless churches and joining Holiness and Pentecostal churches that accepted passionate service, singing, and welcomed female soloists and female evangelists?

One of these so-called "silk-stocking" churches was Metropolitan Missionary Baptist Church located on the West Side of Chicago. Its leadership recognized the need to showcase music for the congregation that met their needs. This goal was accomplished through the publication of a worship hymnal, *The Complete Church Hymnal* (Walton, A.R. et. al. 1923). Songs included in the hymnal bore dates of authorship that went back to the late 1800s and early 1900s. Its preface set forth the objective of the collection:

> We have endeavored to select songs that are best known to our Southern people rather than classical standards so often used in hymnal books that are unknown and cannot be appreciated by the masses. It is published with a firm conviction that it will supply a long felt need in the churches of the Southland for the truly devotional old time Southern way that has proven its worth in our Christian worship for the last hundred years or more.

The "Father of Gospel Music"

The "silk stocking church tradition" embodied the social, political, and spiritual set of circumstances that Thomas Andrew Dorsey (1899-1993) faced in the 1920s when he arrived in Chicago, Illinois from Atlanta, Georgia. Dorsey had gained fame there as a nightclub pianist known as "Georgia Tom."

Dorsey was born in Villa Rica, Georgia. His father, a traveling preacher, used props to get his message across to the church congregations on his circuit. His mother was a church organist and Sunday school teacher. She read the Bible daily, led the family in daily worship, and made a point of performing acts of kindness to perfect strangers—sometimes called the spiritual gift of mercy. In an interview in *Inspirational Thoughts*, Professor Dorsey called her a woman with "unquenchable faith."

Thomas Dorsey preferred the dance halls to the church pews. His blues compositions were well-known. His wife Nettie, however, tried unsuccessfully to persuade him to use his talents in service to the Lord. He first converted to Christianity at an annual meeting of the National Baptist Convention in 1921. Professor W.M. Nix's singing of "I Do, Don't You?" impressed Thomas greatly. He wanted to make music like that. Subsequently, he became a pianist at New Hope, a small Baptist church on the South Side of Chicago.

"Gospel Blues"

If there is one person who is responsible for legitimatizing gospel music, it is Professor Thomas A. Dorsey. He is best known for his pioneering work with choirs in Chicago and the founding of his national organization, The National Convention of Gospel Choirs and Choruses in 1933. The formation of gospel choirs at Ebenezer Baptist Church and Pilgrim Baptist Church revolutionized Sunday morning worship and brought gospel music into all churches connected with his ministry and teaching.

"Gospel blues," a term coined by Dorsey to describe the elevation of blues into gospel became acceptable in Northern Protestant churches for the first time in their history. Old-line church pastors in the 1930s felt legitimate in adding gospel music to their worship services. Professor Dorsey, whose influence caused this shift in music ministry, is rightly called the "Father of Gospel Music."

The complex origin of African American music presented many problems for Dorsey when he introduced gospel blues to the established churches of Chicago and the North. Much of the dislike for this type of music stemmed from two sources. One was the obvious similarity of gospel rhythms and vocals to the music of blues halls and Saturday night jazz clubs. The other factor, the role of "caller" that Dorsey developed as a unique gospel style, reminded many pastors of a Southern "bush harbor" religion that did not fit in with the hopes of Northern blacks to assimilate into the dominant white culture. The so-called "silk-stocking" churches preferred Handel and Brahms to gospel music, which was seen as the music of the lower impoverished class. This dilemma was the problem that Dorsey ultimately resolved. Rev. Dorsey stated in the PBS series "We've Come This Far by Faith – Faith Journey Part 3: "Preachers said gospel is preached – not sung. I've been thrown out of some of the best churches in America."

The old-line churches simply felt that Dorsey's music was not suitable for dignified worship services. His purpose for writing religious blues was not to attack old line churches, Dorsey maintained, but to dedicate his musical gift to God. He believed that his talent as a blues musician was meant by God to be used in His service. Dorsey now only wanted to be God's instrument. Said Dorsey, "No, I wasn't trying to change it [church music], but I was just struck with something that would change it over, something that the Lord gave me. He wanted it. He accepted it; I got my authority from God. ("Sing the Gospel," Rise of Gospel Blues TADS, (17) Interview, Jan. 22, 1971, 13)."

A Struggle for Success. The music that Thomas Dorsey wrote and submitted to the National Baptist Convention, however, was not successful initially. The publication of his first two songs was due largely to the effort of Lucie E. Campbell. She served as the musical director of the New Congress of the National Baptist Convention and was very instrumental in the musical development of the National Baptist Convention. Ms. Campbell, as musical director of the New Congress of the National Baptist Convention, helped to set the standards for the music of the National Sunday School and the educational curriculum of the church. Chicago was a center of sacred music–in genre as well as publication. It was second only to New York. Dorsey capitalized on the recognition he received with the publication of his work in *The Gospel Pearls* in 1922. Publication in the *Gospel Pearls* and the *National Baptist Hymnal* launched his eventual rise to national recognition and public acceptance. Two of his published songs in 1924 were "If I Don't Get There" and "We Will Meet Him in the Sweet By and By." The circulation of these two compositions in churches around the country did much to further his music ministry.

A Music Printer and Publisher. In 1925, when Charles Pace and the Pace Jubilee Singers were denied royalties for their music by Victor Phonograph, Professor Dorsey began to print and sell sacred music. Victor Phonograph had denied the group royalties because no printed sheet music existed for the songs. This knowledge helped Dorsey. Later, the Pace Singers asked Dorsey to write their music and print it for them. He hit upon the idea to print his own music this way as well and publish songs.

Dorsey's composition "If You See My Savior," published in 1925, didn't reveal his blues background. He revised it so that it was more readable and usable by "storefront" musicians. Professor Dorsey, using funds from borrowed money, purchased stamps, and mailed "Some Day Somewhere, If You See My Savior" to Baptist churches throughout the country. It took him three years before he received one order. A discouraged Thomas Dorsey was tempted to return to jazz composition full-time.

Merging Gospel with Blues. Thomas Dorsey

didn't assume credit for creating gospel music. Instead, he credits himself with merging gospel with blues. The music he created in the 1930s emerged as solo and choral gospel blues. Dorsey viewed his music as sermonic presentations which he clarified in a 1977 interview:

> Now, I didn't originate the word gospel. I want you to know. I didn't originate that word. Gospel, the word "gospel" has been used down through the ages. But I took the word, took a group of singers, or one singer, as far as that's concerned, and I embellished [gospel],made it beautiful, more noticeable, and more susceptible with runs and trills and moans in it. That's really one of the reasons my folk called it gospel music (Harris, 1992, 151).(Excerpted from TADS, 27, Interview, Jan.18, 1977, 1.255)

An Instant Hit. Rev. E.H. Hall was an evangelistic gospel singer and recording Baptist preacher whom Thomas Dorsey heard sing. Professor Dorsey was impressed with Rev. Hall's style of singing and how he connected with those who heard him sing at revivals. He was the first preacher used by Dorsey to create the "preacher sound" in his compositions. Professor Dorsey made a deal with Rev. Hall and offered to accompany him when he sang at revivals and during his travels. This arrangement was beneficial to both Hall and Dorsey.

Hall also brought Thomas Dorsey to the 1930 National Baptist Convention in Chicago held at the Coliseum. Rev. Hall introduced Thomas Dorsey to other urban evangelists and preachers. The convention, troubled with internal conflict, was still able to boast a 1,000-voice choir. Old-line music directors were in attendance. The convention featured a musical about Baptist history in America complemented by a chorus and a 50-piece orchestra. "Gospels" were performed along with classical music at this convention.

Willie Mae Fisher sang Dorsey's composition "If You See My Savior" during morning devotion. The song was an instant hit. Dorsey hadn't planned to attend the convention at first, but he recognized that the support of Lucie E. Campbell and E.W Isaacs—convention "bigwigs" could advance his music nationally. Professor Dorsey sold more than 4, 000 copies of that song at the 1930 convention. This success prompted Thomas Dorsey to present his songs as sermons (Harris 1992, 179).

The Origin of "Precious Lord, Take My Hand"

Dorsey continued to write gospel music which he sent to churches without success while he supported his family with his earnings from secular blues. A crisis of faith helped him turn from secular music to gospel music wholly in 1932. The origin of Thomas A. Dorsey's most celebrated song *"Precious Lord, Take My Hand"* is legendary. The music poured out of him as he coped with the loss of his beloved wife Nettie and infant son, Thomas Andrew Dorsey, Jr.

In the publication *Thomas Dorsey on the Precious Lord Story & Gospel Songs*, Dorsey later wrote that "I was chosen or destined to do this work from creation. If there is such a thing as reincarnation, I've been on earth before and resumed work where I left off at the previous transition (Dorsey 3)."

Dorsey's wife had tried unsuccessfully before to get him to leave the secular music field and devote himself solely to God. He finally answered the call when, performing on the road, he received the news of the death of his wife during childbirth.

He arrived home that night mourning Nettie's death while rejoicing in the birth of his newborn son. Dorsey held the infant that night, only to witness his death the next day. Dorsey was angry at God. He felt God had done him wrong. He refused to do anything for God: write music or serve Him in churches. He wanted only to go back to performing full-time in jazz clubs. But God intervened and spoke to him directly:

> You are not alone. I tried to speak to
> you before. It was you that should
> have gotten out of the car and not
> gone to St. Louis instead of the oth-
> er man who got out and stayed at
> home. "I said, Thank you, Lord, I un-
> derstand. I'll never make that same
> mistake again." (Dorsey, 4).

He continues by recalling that he went to Madam Malone's Poro College he next Saturday night:

> There in my solitude, I began
> to browse over the keys like a
> gentle herd pasturing on tender turf.

Something happened to me there. I had a strange feeling inside. A sudden calm—a quiet stillness. As my fingers began to manipulate over keys, words began to fall in place on the melody like drops of water falling from the crevice of a rock (Dorsey, 4-5).

Professor Theodore Frye, Director of the Ebenezer Baptist Church Chorus, persuaded him not to change the title of the song to "Blessed Lord." Said Dorsey:

This is the greatest song I have written out of near four hundred gospel songs.... The price exacted for "Precious Lord" was very high. The grief, the sorrow, the loneliness, the loss, the uncertainty of the future, but I was requited or repaid with double dividends and compound interest. The Lord blessed me with another wife Kathryn Dorsey, and two fine children.....I am happy now at 70 years of age (Dorsey 4).

Gospel Music Revolutionized

Dorsey wrote five songs during this period of grief between 1932 and 1933 that revolutionized how gospel compositions were written and sung. Influential people in music ministry whom Dorsey had met through the National Baptist Convention helped him to continue to spread the gospel message in song. Two Baptist preachers of established black old- line churches in Chicago hired him to develop and refine the music ministry of their churches.

Dr. James Howard Smith, new pastor of the Ebenezer Baptist Church in Chicago, hired Thomas Dorsey to bring life back into the church morning worship service. The addition of gospel music revitalized the congregation. Professor Dorsey and the gospel choir of Ebenezer accompanied Pastor Smith of Ebenezer to the anniversary service of Rev. Junious C. Austin at Pilgrim Baptist Church in February 1932. Dr. Austin was encouraged by the success and acceptance of gospel music at Ebenezer. He asked Thomas Dorsey to organize the charter gospel choir at Pilgrim Baptist Church in 1932 (Harris, 1992).

The success of gospel music in these old-line churches legitimatized gospel blues. This music was heard in more mainstream black churches by the mid 1930s. The spiritual message and widespread acceptance of "Precious Lord" in black churches was important in securing gospel music's newfound favor. Moreover, the acceptance of Dorsey's music by two respected and well-known Baptist church pastors lent his music acceptance and approval.

Dorsey's Musical Partnerships

Thomas Dorsey expanded his partnerships to include evangelists who incorporated his "sermons in song" with their preaching. One of them, Sallie Martin, loved to sing the gospel, and she helped popularize Dorsey's gospel message and music in her travels throughout the country as a soloist. Professor Dorsey had trained her to perform the gospel blues in the style (preacher sound) he arranged. Thomas Dorsey, in his lifetime, is credited with having written and published more than 400 songs. Who better to sing them than evangelist Sallie Martin, a singer who spoke her songs and preached their message?

Dorsey's and Martin's partnership lasted until 1939. She organized choruses in cities to which she traveled and built a network of singers. Sallie Martin was aware of the potential of Dorsey's music. She tried to convince him of the opportunity that it presented, but he was not interested in expanding his reach during that time. Martin then formed a joint music publishing company with Kenneth Morris in 1939. Nonetheless, she and Dorsey collaborated to formalize the independent state choruses into the National Convention of Gospel Choirs and Choruses in 1933.

Mahalia Jackson. Mahalia Jackson and a trio of brothers, the Johnson Singers, began singing in Chicago in 1928. Their style of singing was known to either offend or endear them to pastors. The Johnson Singers performed in established churches as well as in storefront churches.

Dorsey heard Mahalia Jackson sing during the time he was working with Sallie Martin. He envisioned the blending of blues with the spirit and message of gospel. Jackson often appeared at revival services at Pilgrim Baptist Church, where Dorsey had formed his charter gospel choir. She also sang for hospital and home visitation ministries and became part of the first radio singing group formed by Dorsey, the "University Radio Singers." In 1932, she joined the Pilgrim Gospel Chorus.

Mahalia Jackson became the best-known gospel singer of her time. She performed throughout the world. Gospel music gained worldwide legitimacy and acceptance through her ambassadorship of song. She was show-cased by politicians as well as pastors and often delivered a personal testimony along with her songs, clapping her hands and patting her feet to the inspirational messages they conveyed. Mahalia Jackson was the original "Queen of Gospel Music," a title later given to Albertina Walker by James Cleveland.

Albertina Walker. Mahalia Jackson intro-duced Professor Dorsey to Albertina Walker, who had visited Pilgrim just to observe him there in his role of music minister. In Decem-ber 1993, Walker stated in an interview with the *Chicago Tribune* that Chicago had always been the place to preach the gospel [in song]. She grew up in West Point Baptist Church, her church home until her death in 2010. Her entire life was one of music ministry – from the children's to adult choir. Said Walker:

> As a youngster, I used to listen to all the great gospel singers who came to my church to sing – Sally Martin, Ro-berta Martin, Mahalia Jackson, and Professors Frye and Thomas Dorsey, who were choral directors and sing-ers....gospel singers everywhere sing

[Dorsey's] music.

James Mundy, an old-line choir director gave this explanation for Thomas Dorsey's gospel music popularity. "The Negro peo-ple liked gospel 'cause it goes back to Africa. That's why it got a hold of them. It's indig-enous (Harris 180)."

Gospel Choirs Spread

Gospel choirs spread rapidly throughout the black church after 1932. They were organized in the Baptist, Sanctified, and Church of God in Christ "Negro districts of Chicago." Resistance to "jazz gospel hymns," nonetheless still bubbled beneath the surface in some church circles. The Chicago Defender, in 1932, credited Professor Dorsey; Madame Magnolia Butts, Directress, Metropolitan Community Church Gospel Chorus; and Professor Theodore Frye, Director Ebenezer Baptist Chorus, for initiating the chorus movement. St. Clair Drake wrote about the contributions of these three contributors to the gospel chorus movement in the *Chicago Defender.*

> The gospel chorus movement had its beginning April 1, 1932, when Prof. Thomas A. Dorsey, eminent gospel songwriter, Mme. Magnolia Lewis (Butts) directress, Metropolitan Community Church Gospel chorus; Prof. Theodore Frye, director Ebenezer Baptist Chorus, launched a drive advocating a renaissance of gospel singing in the churches of Chicago (Drake 1940).

A Need to Professionalize the Gospel Music Ministry

Dorsey was called an evangelical songwriter. The "renaissance," of gospel music, resulting from Dorsey's travels and from the urging of his "executive committee," was the impetus for professionalizing the gospel music ministry by founding a national formal organization to serve the needs of gospel singers in nearby states. Thus, the Chicago choruses formed a union of more than 1,500 members. Frye and Butts voted Dorsey president. Choruses had been organized in 24 states as a result of the travels of Dorsey and his committee. Those choruses were invited to Chicago to meet with the Chicago union and to "map out plan and program for the expansion of the organization throughout the country. This organization, in 1934, became the National Convention of Gospel Choirs and Choruses, Inc. Professor Dorsey was voted National Organizer in 1934, and he remained active in the organization until his death (Harris 1992, 256).

The first convention was held at Pilgrim Baptist Church from August 30 to September 1, 1933. Dorsey, by then, had become regarded as "the race's greatest gospel songwriter." He shared his major objectives for the convention:

> I recommend that the gospel singers of this national convention have a home or headquarters, with departments to study, rehearse and develop the highest type of gospel singing with the very best interpretation of the spirituals and heart songs (Harris 1992, 267).

He also envisioned the headquarters as a way station for gospel singers when traveling through the city on engagements and that it adhere to the standard of a Christian home, a place to shape the young singer and to help the older one to reach his highest potential.

The National Convention of Gospel Choirs and Choruses

The stated mission of the National Convention of Gospel Choirs and Choruses has remained true to the legacy of Thomas A. Dorsey to this day. Bishop Kenneth H. Moales, president, succeeded Dr. Dorsey and led the organization until his death in 2010. The aim of the National Convention of Gospel Choirs and Choruses is to "better the Christian Singer, instrumentalist, educator or leader; to enable the prepared gospel ambassador, and to spiritually motivate everyone to live the message of the gospel song. Our goal is to foster an appreciation of gospel music and to develop the spiritual growth of our membership *(www.ncgcc.com)*."

Dorsey endeavored to impress upon the established and often resentful members of the senior choirs of the NCGC's constituent churches that the National Convention of Gospel Choirs and Choruses was more than a group of enthusiastic singers. Therefore, he invested considerable time in their vocal development,   accepting anyone who had a "sincere desire to sing and praise God. Three questions he posed to potential mentees were:

- Do you want to sing?
- Do you belong to the Church?
- Do you have a personal relationship with God?   He could train their voices if they met those criteria. (Harris 1992, 266)

Dorsey set forth these expectations for gospel music in a pamphlet "Improving the Music in the Church," published in 1949 by Kenneth Morris. These views were expressed in the Smithsonian Institute's tribute to Dr. Dorsey in 1985 in the program *Classic Gospel Song.*

> ...when it comes to the ministry of music in the church, I think it should not be too stiff, too classical, or too jazzy... I find some (choirs) who do not possess enough spirit and others who have too many embellishments that are mistaken for 'spirit'... loud vociferous singing, uninspired gesticulations, or self-encouraged spasms of the body is not spirit.... I don't believe in going to get the spirit before it comes.

The Model for the Gospel Movement in America. The National Convention of Gospel Choirs and Choruses was the model for the gospel movement in America. Gospel music had evolved from what was considered a primitive expression of slave music and an adaptation of the blues, often described as "devil's music," into a respected Black sacred song. A new style of worship in black churches had now been firmly established where the "caller" female soloist was an integral part of all worship services. Harris (1992) states that "the female caller was introduced into 'white-stocking' churches as gospel blues. It contained the 'bush harbor' spirit. It was a witness to the former music of enslavement. The bush harbor meeting became institutionalized within the black church (250, 251)." Spirituals had also shared in the transmutation of the bush harbor meeting to the established black church. Personal identification with an outward expression of faith and joy had become accepted as a demonstrative public expression of praise to God.

Dorsey was recognized publicly as the "Father of Gospel Music" at the 49th annual Convention of Gospel Choirs and Choruses held in 1992, the year before his death in his hometown of Chicago. A frail Dorsey was last seen by a large audience in 1982 at the 39th Annual Convention of Choirs and Choruses, which took place in St. Louis, Missouri. He walked up the aisle dressed in white, the color he adopted for the opening consecration service at the convention. The convention highlights were narrated by one of his protégés, Evangelist Willie Mae Ford Smith, for the documentary "Say Amen Somebody." This documentary was later reissued in January 2007 as a DVD directed by George T. Nierenberg.

Rev. Dorsey recounted how God spoke to his heart: "The voice of God whispered, 'you need to change.'" He recalled the words of Sallie Martin, his business manager, who was a driving force in the convention as well: "Sing the song; sell the music afterwards."

Dorsey was most proud of the impact his music had on peoples' lives. He said that he took discarded people and made a way for them to sing to the glory and honor of God. He sang of his hope and faith in the song, "When I've Done the Best." He declared that he intended to live on the Lord's shoulders for many, many, many moons.

The Death of Thomas A. Dorsey

Thomas A. Dorsey died on January 23, 1993 at his home in Chicago. His homegoing service was held at Pilgrim Baptist Church on January 29. People from all walks of life paid tribute to this great man of God. Lisa Collins, in an article in *Billboard* entitled "Gospel Pioneer Thomas A. Dorsey Dies: Father of Gospel Music," wrote these words to commemorate his legacy in gospel music:

> Thomas A. Dorsey dies.... he was a great choir director. Albertina Walker went to churches just to watch him direct. No one could bring the music, lyrics, and sound from a choir that he could. His songs brought a beat that everybody could identify with and through which they could really deliver the sentiment that was gospel. He defined the true essence of gospel music... he embodied it (80, 2-6).

A Public Tribute. A tribute to Thomas A. Dorsey, "Father of Gospel Music," was held after his death at the Harold Washington Center Auditorium of the Chicago Public Library. Sid Ordower, host of the "Jubilee Showcase," who helped to put gospel artists on the map in Chicago during the 1960s, donated 100 of the tapes from his long-running show to the Chicago Public Library for transfer to VHS format. They represent the most comprehensive collection of gospel video in America. Ordower credits Dorsey with sending him his first fan letter in 1963. In a January 25, 1993 *Chicago Tribune* article, Ordower offered these words: "That music of his was so beautiful that it actually brought people into the church. That's the sign of a great composer."

The tribute featured film clips of Dorsey accompanying John Sellars and Delois Barrett Campbell and the Barrett Sisters. The collection included the Soul Stirrers, Inez Andrews and the New Friendship Baptist Church Choir, Jessy Dixon and the Jessy Dixon Singers, and James Cleveland and the Cleveland Singers. Other gospel greats included on the tapes are Albertina Walker, the Norfleet Brothers, and saxophonist Arthur Scales. Wrote *Chicago Sun Times* reporter Cheryl Jenkins Richardson in the article "Gospel: A Tribute Fit for a Legend," in February 1, 1993: the tribute to Dorsey culminated in the audience's participation in singing his classic "Precious Lord."

Tributes from Dorsey's Peers. Mahalia Jackson reflected on her experiences throughout the years working with Thomas Dorsey in a tribute for the National Museum of American History:

> When (Dorsey) began to write gospel music, he still had a happy beat in his songs. They're sung by thousands of people... who believe religion is a joy....Professor Dorsey would have copies of his wonderful songs along with him when we traveled together and he would sell them for ten cents apiece to the folks who wanted to own them.

Roebuck "Pop" Staples, father of the legendary gospel group The Staples Singers said in a January 31, 1993 *Chicago Tribune* article:

> I think his songs will go on forever because they touched both white and black....They're about something sacred, about everything that has been, and everything that will be. They're as fresh now as they were 50 years ago because they're about everybody.

Evangelist Shirley Caesar reflected on his life as a teacher and a mentor:

> ...had it not been for him, there could have never been a Mahalia Jackson, or Rev. James Cleveland. Just his being allowed us to not have to plow through anything. If not for him, I would not be able to sing and jump and dance like I do. He suffered to pave the way for us. I doubt if we could ever run into anybody who could write hymns like that. One of the greatest gospel songwriters of all time has fallen asleep (Collins, 80).

In March 1993, Tom Granger wrote in *Contemporary Christian Music:*

> Though his talent at the piano was always prodigious, I think Thomas A. Dorsey is an excellent example of 'being faithful in the little things.' He gave his gifts back to the One who gave them so freely, and in time they were multiplied
> beyond his own imagining (4).

Doris Dorsey, reflecting on her father's life stated: "His biggest accomplishment was that he was recognized as the "Father of Gospel

Music" and that he lived to get the recognition (Collins 80)."

A year after his death, the 1993 National Convention of Gospel Choirs and Choruses celebrated the life and legacy of Thomas A. Dorsey. Its theme was "A Gospel Pilgrimage Back to Pilgrim."

Accolades and Awards

Although he was recognized in 1976 as the winner of the National Music Award, Thomas Dorsey was largely ignored by the media for many years before his death. He was snubbed by the RIAA (The Recording Industry Association of America), and, despite its having been translated into more than 50 languages, "Precious Lord" isn't included in the Grammy Hall of Fame. Composers attribute this oversight to mistaken identity, since some believe he was confused with a jazzman of the same name. Ironically, the gospel music industry itself, which he helped to found, was strangely silent in awarding him honors.

The documentary "Say Amen Somebody" (1983), which chronicled Dorsey's life and was narrated by one of the evangelists he influenced, Willie Mae Ford Smith, was nominated for an Academy Award. Professor Dorsey was also the recipient of three honorary doctorates and became the first black musician voted into the Gospel Music Association Hall of Fame in 1982. Dorsey, somewhat belatedly, was honored in 1992 with a special Grammy for lifetime achievement. Professor Dorsey became an ordained minister of the gospel in the 1960s.

The Legacy of Thomas Andrew Dorsey

Thomas Dorsey's musical legacy has been compared to that of one of our greatest lawyers. Jerry Adler, a columnist in *Newsweek*, compares the lives of Supreme Court Justice Thurgood Marshall and Thomas A. Dorsey:

> One man made earthly law better. Another made God's law sing Adler continued by saying, "from 30,000 churches across the land every Sunday, voices are raised in the music he put there, the words of salvation improbably joined to the rhythms of blues and stride piano to create the sound he called gospel (February 8, 1993, 56)."

Marcus Hampton wrote in *Score Magazine*: "From a seed of bondage to a tree of spiritual knowledge, the legacy of gospel music was born (January-February 1993, 12)."

Dorsey received more accolades from composer and multi-Grammy winner Edwin Hawkins, gospel singer, and director in the documentary "We've Come This Far by Faith –Faith Journey, Part 3 (PBS).

Professor Dorsey is recognized as the "Father of Contemporary Gospel Music." He is credited with composing more than 1,000 songs (*Billboard*, February, 1993), and is cited for "virtually creating the modern gospel style, reshaping the older Black religious tradition into a twentieth century expression (Roach 1992, 98)."

Thomas Dorsey changed the character and composition of church services and gospel music ministry in the black church forever.

Kathryn Dorsey, his widow, said in an interview on January 28, 2011 that after his wife Nettie died, he did nothing but gospel. "Gospel music is a gift from God; it brings people to God. That's what it's all about," Dorsey's widow said. She wondered why God didn't give her a gift or talent for music, but acknowledged the gift God did give her –that of encouragement, which she gave to her husband during their marriage. She still attends the annual tributes in Chicago that celebrate his life and legacy.

Professor Dorsey's legacy to gospel music is a testament to his commitment to live his life for God after the death of his first wife and son. His grace gifts in music ministry will continue to inspire and uplift countless individuals for all time.

Thomas A. Dorsey, the "Father of Gospel Music".
Photo courtesy of his daughter Doris Dorsey, 1973.

Chapter Three:

Gospel Music to End of the Twentieth Century

"We shall overcome. We shall overcome. We shall overcome
someday. Down in my heart, I do believe.
We shall overcome, someday...."
—Rev. Charles A. Tindley

W illiam R. Fuqua, gospel historian, categorizes twentieth-century gospel musicians and performers into the classical gospel era, the modern gospel era, or the contemporary gospel era. Gospel music began in the 20th century as an expression of the theology of black people through music. He recalls how gospel music was categorized as "the devil's music" as he grew up in Columbus, Georgia. He wasn't allowed to play this music.

Elder Fuqua stated..."during my younger years, I was not allowed to play gospel music at the elementary, high school, or college and university levels. It was frowned upon in sophisticated Baptist, Catholic, Methodist, and Episcopal churches. I had to play classical, hymns, anthems, spirituals, and popular music in public (Fuqua 1997)."

Elder Fuqua began his gospel music collection in the 1950s. The gospel music that was heard on the radio could be purchased by interested listeners. Elder Fuqua states, "If you bought a 78, 45, or 33 1/3 recording, you could also buy the music. This was very educational. The prices ranged from ten cents to thirty-five cents for music (Fuqua 1997)."

The lack of written gospel history has frustrated Elder Fuqua throughout the years. His zeal for collecting the original music and history was for future generations. "It is important," he stresses, "that they see the music and the words." Music purchased today doesn't have the sheet music that accompanies the songs. This gospel music heritage is important, therefore, as a legacy for musicians and gospel artists of the 21st century.

Elder Fuqua lists several of the professional gospel music groups who toured in the 1950s and the 1960s. These singers sung wherever they were invited. The venues varied from small churches, tabernacles, and auditoriums to concert halls (Fuqua).

He places the following gospel greats in the classical gospel era of the 1930s to the 1940s: Thomas A. Dorsey, Kenneth Morris, Theodore Frye, Doris Akers, Bessie Griffin, Rosetta Tharpe, W. H. Brewster Sr., Lucie Campbell, Sallie Martin, Willie Mae Ford Smith, Mahalia Jackson, Roberta Martin, the Angelic Gospel Singers, and the Pace Singers. These singers and musicians were the forerunners of the modern and contemporary gospel eras (Fuqua, 5). They were trailblazers and pioneers in gospel music ministry.

The modern gospel era encompasses the 1950s to the mid-1960s. This period has also been termed "The Golden Age of Gospel." This era introduced quality choirs, quartets—a cappella and electronic—and soloists to audiences through tours, concerts, and recordings. Ensembles performed with piano and/or organ. This style of gospel singing remained virtually unchanged until the mid-1980s. The following names were among the famous gospel soloists, composers, and groups of the 1950s and 1960s: The Sally Martin Singers; The Ward Singers featuring Clara Ward and Marian Williams; The Roberta Martin Singers; The Davis Sisters featuring Ruth Davis; The Caravans featuring Albertina Walker and Shirley Caesar; the Gospel Harmonettes featuring Dorothy Love Coates; The Dixie Hummingbirds; The Soul Stirrers featuring Sam Cooke; The Staples Singers featuring Mavis and Pop Roebuck Staples; The Angelic Gospel Singers featuring Mrs. Allison; Raymond Rasberry; A. J. Twiggs; Robert Anderson; Willie Webb; E.B. Smallwood; Inez Andrews; R.H. Goodpasteur; The Mighty Clouds of Joy; Thurston G. Frazier; Little Lucy Matthews; Rev. Milton Brunson and The Thompson Community Singers; Little Sammie Bryant; L. M. Bowles; The O'Neal Twins; The Boyer Brothers; George Jordan with First Church of Deliverance, Rev. Clarence Cobb, Pastor; The Original Baltimore Echoes – Metropolitan (Kansas); Elder William R. Fuqua; the Original Chapter of the Columbus/Phoenix City Choral Union; Dr. Margaret Douroux; Twinkie and the Clark Sisters; The Williams Brothers; Tramaine Hawkins; James Cleveland; Thomas Whitfield and Company; The Lawrence Robert Singers; the Isaac Douglas Singers; Rev. Clay Evans and Fellowship

Baptist Church; Stars of Faith; Maceo Woods and the Christian Tabernacle Choir; the Barrett Sisters featuring Delois Barrett; Cosmopolitan Church of Prayer, Father Hayes Pastor; Donald Vails and The Choraleers; The Clefs; The Charles Fold Singers; Al Green; Louise McCord; Thelma Houston; The Swan Silvertones; The Pilgrim Travelers; The Five Blind Boys of Alabama; The Alex Bradford Singers; Della Reese; Cassietta George, and others.

The 1950s and 1960s was an extremely fruitful period in gospel music, filled by an abundance of people involved in music ministry with voice and/or instrument (Fuqua, 6-7).

Secular music was more rewarding financially to some artists who began their careers in gospel music ministry. Successful cross-over artists include Sam Cooke of the Soul Stirrers; Dinah Washington of the Sallie Martin Singers; Dionne Warwick of the Drinkard Singers; Thelma Houston of the Art Reynolds Singers; Wynona Carr; Rev. Al Green; Mavis and Roebuck Staples of the Staple Singers; "Little" Esther Phillips; Aretha Franklin; and others (Fuqua, 8).

The perseverance of the early gospel greats in the face of tremendous odds paved the way for the success of those in the contemporary gospel era. Some gospel artists were able to continue gospel careers in both modern and contemporary eras. These included Edwin Hawkins and the Edwin Hawkins Singers; Walter Hawkins and the Love Center Choir; James Cleveland with the Southern California Community Choir; Andrae Crouch and the Disciples; Sara Jordan Powell; Jessy Dixon; Shirley Caesar; Billy Preston; and others (Fuqua, 11).

Contemporary gospel today includes rap and holy hip-hop. Notable names in this present era include Kirk Franklin and the Family; God's Property; Angie and Debbie; Be Be and Ce Ce Winans; The Clark Sisters; The Winans; Marvin Sapp; John P. Kee; Fred Hammond and Radicals for Christ; Men of Standard; Special Gift; Daniel Winans; Yolanda Adams; Vanessa Bell Armstrong; Vicki Winans; Dottie Peoples; Commissioned; Donnie McClurkin; Kurt Carr; and others (Fuqua, 12).

Indeed, it would be impossible to recognize all of those who were influential in gospel music history. Albertina Walker loved to say that she and others stood on the shoulders of those who had come before them—trailblazers who endured many indignities as they performed around the country.

Gospel Music during the Civil Rights Era

Music is the birthright of a people. It transmits cultures and values and provokes emotions that both soothe and enrage. It describes the determination of a people who have survived the pain of struggle and oppression. The music of the Civil Rights Movement was transforming. Gospel music became a unifying force for Americans during the Civil Rights Era and helped sound the call to social action.

Social justice was intertwined with religious responsibility as churches became involved in the Civil Rights Movement, beginning with the 1950s but reaching its height during the decade of the 1960s. Music became a vehicle of social action that expressed the needs of a people while magnifying the injustices prevalent in society. Many of the songs that were performed were reminiscent of the spirituals sung during slavery that functioned as code songs for the oppressed.

Gospel as Folk Music. The PBS documentary "Freedom Songs" called black music the origin of American folk music. The documentary traced the influence of spirituals on the Civil Rights Movement. Andrew Young, former Mayor of Atlanta, and former U.S. ambassador to the U.N., spoke of the freedom riders and the use of music to inspire and mobilize support for the movement. Gospel music was seen as the genesis of that genre of music. Spiritual music was described as "the soul of the movement." The songs encouraged the freedom riders when they were arrested, beaten, and jailed in several Southern cities. Gospel music was also referred to as "the soundtrack of the soul" and was of vital importance in the struggle for equal rights. Black music throughout the history of blacks in America had always delved into the themes of freedom, oppression and salvation ("Sing for Freedom,"1990).

Freedom Songs. The freedom riders sang the songs in jail to build solidarity when they were deprived of food and water. Many songs were composed spontaneously by those in the Movement. Words were put to familiar tunes. The messages elevated the struggle from the physical realm to the spiritual realm and made it easier for the oppressed riders to endure the physical cruelty of those opposing freedom for all people.

Freedom songs were sung by both religious and secular groups. The Movement was empowered by the energy it received from black musical roots. Many songs, such as Sam Cooke's "A Change is Going to Come," The Impressions' "People Get Ready," as well as songs by Mavis Staples, Otis Redding, Jerry Butler, Freedom Riders, and a variety of country singers expressed through music, the sentiments of the people for change and equality.

Gospel Music and Social Justice. Gospel music had become the means of expression for black people not only in church settings of corporate praise and worship, or in private periods of personal meditation, but now also for a social justice movement. The gospel music organizations formed by Professor Dorsey in the 1930s and later by James Cleveland in the 1960s were the vehicles for petitioning God in song concerning the issues of the times. During this time James Cleveland visited the University of California's Berkeley campus, a hotbed of social protest during the 1960s. Rev. Cleveland wed gospel and pop when he performed in 1970 before black militant students at Berkeley.

Social and spiritual consciousness merged as people throughout the country—irrespective of race and creed—united to demand a better America for themselves and their progeny. Networks were established throughout the country–connecting groups, choirs, choruses, unions, soloist, quartets, churches, and chapters. Gospel musicians and gospel artists utilized their gifts and talents during this period in our history, and the music of the Southern protestors and organizers was gospel music. Composers wrote songs both independently and in churches and in groups as marchers walked, protested at sit-ins, and led peaceful demonstrations. SCLC and Dr. Martin Luther King Jr. were at the forefront of these demonstrations to demand the equal rights and acceptance that blacks were still denied since they first arrived on these shores. It was during this time of social upheaval in America that Cleveland's dream for developing and promoting his concept for the gospel genre of a music organization was born. That vision became the Gospel Music Workshop of America.

"We Shall Overcome." White folk artists joined black gospel singers and musicians in spreading the message of equality. Black gospel music, particularly, the song that became known as the Movement's protest song, "We Shall Overcome," was the anthem for grassroots organizations in the South. Journalists who covered the boycotts and strikes wrote and recorded the music of black people. These songs were popularly known as "message songs." Their crossover appeal was viewed as a way to achieve the harmony and equality African-Americans were seeking.

The turmoil caused by the assassinations of John F. Kennedy, Malcolm X, Dr. Martin Luther King, Jr. and Robert Kennedy ended any hopes of peaceful cultural integration. Blacks however, throughout the country, continued to buy, perform, and sing gospel music.

Rev. James A. Cleveland, Heir to the Dorsey Legacy

Rev. James Cleveland was birthed at a pivotal point in gospel music ministry. He was also fortunate to live in Chicago, the acknowledged Mecca of gospel music. This afforded him the opportunity to be mentored by such gospel music pioneers as Sallie Martin, Professor Thomas A. Dorsey, Mahalia Jackson, and Albertina Walker. Moreover, he had access to extraordinary directors, vocalists, and choirs and was surrounded by powerful preachers whose churches afforded numerous opportunities to hear the gospel preached and sung. Cleveland's early association with Professor Dorsey would give him the experience and insight he needed to develop his own musical organization, and his partnership with Albertina Walker would span three decades in the field of gospel music.

Birth and Early Years. James A. Cleveland was born during the Great Depression in Chicago, Illinois, on December 5, 1931. He was one of three children born to Ben and Rosie (Lee) Cleveland. He worked as a child to help his father with expenses by becoming a paperboy. That was how he met Mahalia Jackson. Said Cleveland:

> I'd go over to her apartment on Indiana Avenue and leave her paper and then put my ear to the door to try to hear her singing. If she wasn't at home, I'd go over to her beauty shop—she used to be a hairdresser you know–and just sit around there

and listen to her hum songs while she was straightening hair (Carpenter, 2005, 87-88).

Cleveland's love for the piano manifested itself at the age of five. He built his "pretend" piano on the windowsill of the family apartment. His family couldn't afford to give him lessons, so he invented a way to learn how to play. He had a keen ear for music and taught himself to play by ear. He was fascinated by the playing of Roberta Martin, the gifted pianist at Pilgrim Baptist Church, and would imitate her style on his "practice piano." Roberta Martin later published the first song, at age 16, he had ever written. It was entitled "Grace Is Sufficient." (*Ebony* November 1968, 14).

Formative Years in the Church. Cleveland attended church services with his grandmother at Pilgrim Baptist Church, where she was a choir member. He accompanied her to rehearsals and eventually became the choir mascot. As a result, he was able to learn the choir songs and sang them during rehearsals.

Thomas Dorsey, Minister of Music at Pilgrim, heard James sing one day. Dorsey, impressed by his voice, wrote a song for him to sing as a soloist called "All I Need Is Jesus." Cleveland remembers standing on a box at the young age of eight and singing before the church in what was described as a beautiful soprano voice. His training as a pianist was furthered under the coaching of Professor Dorsey and Little Lucy Smith.

Cleveland recalled in an interview with Anthony Heilbut: "...I used to practice each night right there on the windowsill. I took those wedges and crevices and made me some black and white keys. And, Baby, I played just like Roberta [Martin]. By the time I was in high school, I was some jazz pianist (Heilbut 1985, 191)."

He joined the gospel group the Thorne Crusaders as a teen and lost his soprano voice as he matured. The strain of trying to compensate for this loss led to the gruff, raspy voice that later became his trademark. Now a baritone, he proudly referred to himself as the "Louis Armstrong of Gospel Music," comparing his voice to a foghorn (191). He compensated for the sound of his voice by singing with superior male sopranos backing him.

The Drive to Succeed. Cleveland worked hard and hustled to achieve success. A *Chicago Tribune* obituary dated February 10, 1991 referenced Rev. Cleveland in an earlier interview with the *Los Angeles Times* in 1990. In the interview, he stated that he got started in the music industry by watching Mahalia Jackson and others perform.

> I'd stand around by the door and hope somebody's musician didn't show up. Then I'd offer to play for them. They'd ask me, "Boy, can you play such-and-such"? And I'd always say I could—even if I never heard of it before in my life. Then they'd say, "All right. I need it in E flat". And I'd go right out there and start playing.

Early Musical Influences

Roach (1992, 97-101) identifies the following artists as pivotal forces in James Cleveland's musical growth and development: Inez Andrews, Shirley Caesar, Dorothy Love Coates, Roberta Martin, Sally Martin, Kenneth Morris, Rev. Cleophas Robinson, Rev. C.L. Johnson, Bessie Griffin, Clarence Fountain, Rev. Clevant Derricks, Harold Smith, Willie Mae Ford, Gloria Spencer, Rosetta Tharpe, Albertina Walker, Clara Ward, Marion Williams, and Pearl William Jones.

Cleveland was influenced by the jazz styles of Louis Armstrong and Dinah Washington as much as he was by Eugene Smith, another member of the Roberta Martin Singers. Robert Anderson of the same group also influenced Cleveland (Heilbut 1985). He recorded a gospelized version of Ray Charles's "Hallelujah, I Love Him So" with the singer in 1959.

On the Move

Cleveland moved frequently during his early years in music ministry, enabling him to meet a variety of musicians, singers and pastors. He moved several times within a ten-year period, and also between several different gospel groups. When Cleveland left Chicago for New York, he was appointed Minister of Music at Faith Temple Church of God in Christ under Bishop A. A. Child.

While in New York, he became a member of the Gospel Allstars of Brooklyn. He later joined Norsalus McKissick and Bessie Folk, former members of the Roberta Martin Singers, in Philadelphia to form the trio The Gospelaires in 1950. These relationships proved to be vital in fulfilling his vision for his own music organization.

Detroit also had a major impact on Cleveland. The city was well known for its great singers and musicians, both secular and religious. Alma Hendrix Parham was most influential in Detroit. She had her own music studio, "Alma and Carl's Home of Music," where she taught piano, organ, and vocal music. Her gift as a directress was legendary. Mrs. Parham published music for others on her own press. Mattie Moss Clark, a nationally known choir director affiliated with the Church of God in Christ became one of the first instructors for the Gospel Music Workshop of America. Mrs. Clark mentored many gospel artists as well as her daughters who are all evangelists and/or singers.

Detroit was home to many gospel artists and musicians. Cleveland relied on a great number of them to help him develop the vision for his gospel music organization. Detroit greats included: Rance Allen; the Fantastics; Bill Moss and The Celestials; The Howard Lemon Singers; The Lucille Lemon Singers; The Mighty Voices of Thunder; The Voices of Tabernacle Choir, with Rev. Charles Ashley Craig, Sr.; The Meditation Singers; Harold Smith and The Majestics; Thomas Whitfield and Company; Bertha Harris; Rev. Robert Grant; Herbert Pickard; Nate Edwards; Dorothy Grant; Leslie Bush; Alfred Bolden; Herbert Pickard; The Eberhart Singers; and Rev. Charles Nicks Jr., with The St. James Young Adult Choir (Fuqua, 10).

While in Detroit, Cleveland became Minister of Music for Rev. C.L. Franklin of the New Bethel Baptist Church in 1951. At the time, he lived with Rev. Franklin and taught young nine-year-old Aretha how to play his chords. Years later, he returned to Detroit and formed a gospel group with Aretha's sister Erma and two other girls (*Jet* October 1967, 49). Cleveland also worked with the talented Craig brothers, members of the Meditation Singers of Detroit (Heilbut 1985).

Return to Chicago. When Cleveland returned to Chicago, he worked with Roberta Martin and the Roberta Martin Singers. Albertina Walker was next, enlisting him to collaborate with her group The Caravans in 1954. "Queen" Walker was very instrumental to his success as a gospel artist—so much so that she refused to record in the studio until he was allowed to sing with her group. Cleveland played piano, wrote songs, and sometimes narrated hymns for them during their concerts. His arrangements made them want to sing, said Walker, though his temperament often caused problems, resulting in his joining and quitting the group many times.

Cleveland organized The Gospel Chimes in 1959. The Chicago group featured Dorothy Norwood, a friend of Cleveland's from the Caravans. Other members of the group included Lee Charles, Claude Timmons, Jessy Dixon, and Imogene Green of the Allstars (Heilbut 1985).

A Second Stay in Detroit. Cleveland's second stay in Detroit (1960) involved collaboration with Rev. Charles Ashley Craig, Sr., at Prayer

Tabernacle, a church that Cleveland, Craig, and Rev. Leslie Bush organized with Cleveland serving as Minister of Music. The association resulted in Cleveland's first recording with the two ministers. The 100-voice choir, the "Voices of Tabernacle," on Hob Records, recorded the instant hit, "The Love of God" in 1960. The song was notable for its modern gospel sound (Heilbut 1985).

Cleveland's collaboration with friends on the East Coast was also fruitful. He was invited to record with Rev. Lawrence Robert's Angelic Choir in Nutley, New Jersey, in the mid-1960s. The music from these associations finally brought national fame and success, recognition that had eluded Cleveland for so long. He testified to God's Providence by acknowledging his newfound fame during a concert rehearsal at the Apollo Theater with the Gospel Allstars in 1960. He declared before an admiring public:

> God is a wonder worker. When I look back sixteen years ago...
> I went to church one night; I wasn't nothing but a poor boy wearing tennis sneakers. I'm glad Albertina's here because she knows what I'm talking about (Darden 212).

Cleveland signed a recording contract with Savoy Records in 1961 upon the release of the albums that featured the Allstars and the Chimes. *California Bound.* In 1962, Cleveland relocated again, this time to California to look for a job, find a church where he could preach, and take a brief hiatus from gospel music.

Many gospel artists were moving West at the time, forming a gospel community. When Cleveland arrived in January 1962, he performed in a gospel concert. Musicologists believe its success was probably the deciding factor that deterred him from crossing over into secular music. That experience also is credited with influencing him to discontinue the traditional gospel legacy that he had inherited from Thomas Dorsey's choir and forge his own unique style of gospel. The result was the group, the James Cleveland Singers, organized in 1963.

A Pastor and Director

Cleveland heeded the call to the ministry and became an ordained minister in the early 1960s. He pastored the New Greater Harvest Baptist Church in Los Angeles, California, before organizing the Cornerstone Institutional Baptist Church, also in Los Angeles, with 60 charter members (November, 1970). Cornerstone was the church that broadened the impact of his music. He accepted no salary as pastor from the church. His sermons and music were "part Baptist and part Sanctified" (Heilbut 1985). It was here also that his protégé, Billy Preston, introduced Mick Jagger to gospel music. Cleveland recorded two sermons, "God Is Not Dead" and God's Promises," as well as three solo albums as pastor of Cornerstone Institutional Baptist Church.

The church quickly outgrew its 2,000-seat capacity. Two church services were needed to accommodate the large congregation. The church grew from a membership of 100 to more than 7,000 during his pastorate, necessitating a move to a larger facility. An April 1984 article in *Ebony Magazine* reported that Rev. Cleveland supervised the renovation of an old supermarket into a beautiful church edifice. There were more than 7,000 members at Cornerstone when Rev. Cleveland died (Boyer 249).

The Southern California Community Choir. The greatest legacy of Cornerstone Institutional Baptist Church was its mass choir—the Southern California Community Choir, also called the James Cleveland Choir —that Cleveland organized in 1969. This choir became one of the dominant choirs of the decade. The group backed Cleveland on his first Grammy Award for "The Ghetto" in 1974, and also on his last Grammy for the recording "Having Church," awarded to Cleveland posthumously in 1991. The choir appeared with him on numerous concerts in the states and abroad.

Heilbut (1985) credits the Southern California Community Choir and the Los Angeles California quartet, the Gospel Cavaliers, with keeping alive the traditional gospel music that was the African American heritage from Albertina Walker and Cassietta George of the Caravans. The Gospel Girls, which included Annette May and two other soloists from the choir, also enjoyed great success in their recordings with Cleveland.

As a testament to his generosity as a musician, Cleveland called on old friends to record with him in California. The collaboration of Rev. Cleveland with the Angelic Choir of

Nutley, New Jersey, and the local choir, the First Baptist Choir of Nutley, New Jersey, was phenomenal. The association resulted in three albums, the second of which featured Billy Preston, a member of the Cleveland Singers, as organist, and James Cleveland alternating between singing, preaching, and chanting. The songs in that series included the hits "How Great Thou Art," "Remember Me," and "Father, I Stretch My Hands to Thee." The best known of the three albums, "Peace Be Still," (1962), is one of the greatest gospel recordings of all time, having sold more than two million copies (Heilbut 1985).

A Style Imitated by Many. Choirs around the country began copying Cleveland's style of music in the 1960s in the same way choirs of the 1930s had imitated Dorsey's style.

Carpenter (2005, 11) writes that [Cleveland]: "laid a foundation for the elevation of choir music into a sophisticated art form....[He] implemented elements of jazz, pop, blues, and sanctified church rhythms ....created a new sound for gospel choirs. His music began to have pop instrumental styles."

Gospel researcher Heilbut remarked that Rev. Cleveland challenged his singers "to reach within themselves to sing his arrangements; his music was full of blues riffs (1985, 217)."

Cleveland instituted the mass choir sound and helped many choirs across the nation record albums. He worked extensively with choirs in Detroit, as well as the Southern California Community Choir. His choirs became known for a certain style of performance writes Mick Brown:

> Music springing on its heels…. In
> it one recognizes one of the corner-
> stones of rock 'n' roll, yet the music
> here bursts with a contagious sense
> of joy and celebration that much con-
> temporary rock seems to have lost al-
> together (Darden 2004, 271).

Cleveland's longevity, spanning the 1960s
to the 1990s, enabled him to dominate the
gospel music industry for more than 30
years. He is credited with producing more
than 45 albums and writing more than 500
songs (*Ebony* November 1968, 82).

Awards and Accolades

Rev. James Cleveland won numerous awards
during his lifetime. He earned a Grammy for
his performance "Live at Carnegie Hall," in
1977 in addition to the aforementioned Grammy he received for the recording "The Ghetto"
in 1974, and his last Grammy for the recording
"Having Church" in 1990. The album recorded
with the Charles Fold Singers of Cincinnati,
Ohio, "Let Me Be an Instrument," garnered
Cleveland his third Grammy in 1980. He always apologized for not being a soloist, even
though one of his solo albums "Live at Carnegie Hall" won a Grammy.

Temple Bible College and Seminary in
Cincinnati, Ohio, awarded him an honorary
doctorate in 1971. The stated honor was "in
recognition of his services and contributions
to the community of God as a religious leader (*Jet*, October 28, 1971, 42).

The Top of the Music Charts. Cleveland's
songs were consistently on *Billboard's* "Soul

Brothers Top Ten Gospel Albums," and the magazine honored him for "Stood on the Banks." His songs were also frequently among *Ebony Magazine's* top gospel music hits. Cleveland's other awards included *Billboard Magazine's* Trend Setters Award, The National Association of Negro Musician's Award, *Ebony Magazine's* Artist Award, and NATRA's (The National Association of Radio and TV Announcers) award for best gospel artist. The latter organization also awarded Cleveland the Golden Mike Award in 1976 for "Lord Do It (*Ebony*, June 1976).

A Star on Hollywood's Walk of Fame. James Cleveland was the first gospel artist to have his star placed on the Hollywood Walk of Fame at Grauman's Chinese Theater in Los Angeles in 1981. This honor was followed by his receiving the NAACP's Image Award for best gospel artist a year later, in 1982. This acclaim freed him to expand his musical interests to operas and films. In addition, he continued to collaborate with secular artists that included Quincy Jones, Dionne Warwick, and Olivia Newton-John. He was chosen to write librettos for Elton John's 1976 opus "Blue Moves."

Cleveland lobbied tirelessly to increase the recognition of gospel music at the Grammy awards. The Stellar Awards, which recognizes the influence of artists in the development and advancement of gospel music, now bestows an annual James Cleveland Lifetime Achievement Award in his honor (*Jet*, 2007). Recipients of the award have included such gospel greats as the Mighty Clouds of Joy,

Albertina Walker, and Richard Smallwood (*Jet*, March 7, 2006).

The Founding of the Gospel Music Workshop of America

Rev. James Cleveland, in the footsteps of his predecessor, Thomas A. Dorsey, leveraged his fame and fortune to achieve his vision for a contemporary organization dedicated to furthering the ministry of gospel music. He now had the time and the means to organize such a project that would be infused with his gifts, talents, and experiences. His participation in The National Convention of Gospel Choirs and Choruses, the gospel music organization formed by Professor Thomas Dorsey and Mrs. Sally Martin in 1934, honed his skills and knowledge of what was required to build and maintain a successful training ground for gospel musicians. The Gospel Music Workshop of America (GMWA) was just the vehicle through which Cleveland could surround himself with the best and brightest that the gospel music industry had to offer. The Gospel Music Workshop of America, Inc., originally known as the Gospel Singers Workshop, grew from a Sing-a-Rama held at C.L. Franklin's New Bethel Baptist Church in Detroit under the direction of Church of God in Christ choir conductress Mattie Moss Clark and Alma Hendricks.

GMWA's First Convention. GMWA's first convention was held August, 1968 in Detroit at the King Solomon Baptist Church and the Masonic Temple (Reese 2004, 11). The new organization grew quickly, and the annual convention became a premier event for the gospel music industry. Convention goers learned Cleveland's new songs and arrangements at the mass choir rehearsals they attended. The songs were then recorded in a "mass choir" arrangement on the closing night of the convention. These albums went on to sell very well. As a result, Savoy Records became known as the "choir company." More than 30 albums have been launched at GMWA conventions, and the organization grew faster than Professor Dorsey's National Convention of Gospel Choirs and Choruses.

Unknown artists' recordings became instant hits after being featured on an album with James Cleveland. He freely welcomed new talent and helped jumpstart the careers of more than 30 gospel recording artists. These talented singers and musicians included Kirk Franklin, Daryl Coley, Donald Lawrence, and John P. Kee. Cleveland considered grooming new talent to be part of his ministry in the field of gospel music.

A Week of Happiness. The annual convention of the GMWA was the subject of an article in *Ebony Magazine* in November 1972. The gospel music week was called "A Week of Happiness," where Rev. Cleveland was known for doing his "holy dance." The article spoke of Rev. Cleveland's expectation for the organization's growth, with his projection that 10,000 persons would attend the following year when the convention was held in Chicago (86).

Journalist Lacy J. Banks wrote in *Ebony Magazine,* in May, 1972 that "gospel music evokes both from its singer and listener the most extreme outpouring of emotion—joyful emotion about trials overcome and about the old dream of someday putting on golden slippers and walking beside the celestial sea. Black gospel music for more than 50 years has been a source of great joy for many people in times of trial, in moments of great trouble (161).

Cleveland's Last GMWA Convention. Rev. James Cleveland attended his last GMWA annual convention in 1990 in Washington, D.C., where he collapsed during the workshop and had to return to Los Angeles to recuperate. Although in poor health, Rev. Cleveland was able to attend an All Star Salute held in his honor at the Dorothy Chandler Pavilion in his adopted hometown of Los Angeles. The tribute commemorated his 50 years in gospel music ministry. Rev. Cleveland, at this time, had won three Grammy Awards for gospel music and accumulated more than a dozen gold albums (*Jet*, November 19, 1990, 56).

As was his habit, Cleveland took advantage of the opportunity to witness to the goodness of God. Reminiscent of Dr. Martin Luther King's "I've Been to the Mountaintop" speech delivered on the night of his death 22 years before, Cleveland may well have known how prophetic his own words would become for him. He told the audience: "If I don't see you again, and if I don't sing again, I'm a witness to the fact that the Lord answers prayer. He let my voice come back to me this morning (*Jet*, February 25, 1991, 50)." It was his last public concert.

Cleveland's Golden Anniversary. Citizen reporter Margaret Mansfield wrote in an article dated November 8, 1990 that Cleveland's golden anniversary featured such gospel legends as Tramaine Hawkins, Sandra Crouch,

The Mighty Clouds of Joy, the Original Caravans, The Williams Brothers, and Walter and Edwin Hawkins and the Hawkins Singers. Secular artists Gladys Knight, Stevie Wonder, and Stephanie Mills were also in attendance. It was Gladys Knight and the Pips' popular version of "You're the Best Thing That Ever Happened to Me" that Cleveland later covered and changed into the gospel song "Jesus Is the Best Thing That Ever Happened to Me." The song remained in the top ten gospel hits from 1976 to 1977. Other artists who paid tribute to him included Daryl Coley and Billy Preston. Andrae Crouch and Walter Hawkins were among those who showed their respect for Rev. Cleveland through their testimonies.

The Death of the James A. Cleveland

Rev. James Cleveland died of heart failure on February 9, 1991 at Brotman Medical Center in Culver City, California. This was less than a year after the gospel salute for his 50 years of gospel music ministry had taken place. His legion of fans paid their respects at a memorial service held in the Los Angeles Shrine Auditorium. Four thousand mourners viewed his open casket in a four-hour service. Mourners included both gospel and secular musicians. Controversy surrounded the details of his death. Disharmony, a frequent aftereffect of the death of a loved one—especially a famous one—did not spare the church body or his heirs (Carpenter, 91).

The "Prince of Gospel Music"

The greatest legacy James Cleveland left was the organization he founded in 1967, The

Gospel Music Workshop of America, Inc. It provided a forum for musicians, vocalists, preachers, and teachers to come together in a nondenominational setting for one week. This organization, still vibrant and growing today, provides opportunities for members to share their gifts and talents, to learn spiritually and professionally, and to offer praise and worship to God. People from all levels of the gospel music industry are embraced. There are more than 28,000 members, with chapters in the United States, the Caribbean, Japan, and Europe.

The GMWA's widespread appeal was underscored by the attendance of a new chapter from Finland at the 2010 convention. The legacy of Rev. James Cleveland to the Gospel Music Workshop of America, Inc., continues to have a major influence on gospel music, gospel artists, and gospel trends.

Cleveland's Gospel Legacy

The Chicago gospel heritage was the social and spiritual environment that nourished a young James Cleveland as he grew into manhood. His music is still played two decades after his death throughout the world. His musical talent inspired vocalists, choirs, songwriters, and musicians to strive for the best within themselves. He urged those in music ministry to do what they do for God. This legacy energized the GMWA, Inc., and his impact on later generations and sub-genres within gospel music remains to this day.

Rev. Cleophas Robinson stated that "the success and survival of gospel music will be secure

as long as the word of God is being preached....
as long as black gospel music is able to uplift
hearts and save even one sinner, it will be the
top music in the world (*Ebony*, May 1972, 168).
A similar sentiment was voiced by Cleveland
himself in an interview in *Jet* Magazine: "Gospel is the music of the black man and it is the
music of the black church....as long as there's a
black church, there's going to be gospel music
(October 22, 1981, 32)."

Dr. Horace Boyer, Professor of Music and
Associate Director of the Fine Arts Center of
the University of Massachusetts, Amherst, is
perhaps the best known researcher on gospel
music history. Said Dr. Boyer: "James Cleveland's gut gospels are included in a short list
of the most profound black cultural products
(Boyer 1995, 226-27)."

"Rev. Marvin Winans remarked, "He could make
you see the song. His love of music and people
was evident." Al Green felt the passion of James
Cleveland by saying, "He brought excitement to
gospel music" (Darden 2004, 271- 273).

Gift of Administration

Rev. James Cleveland experienced success in
nearly every endeavor that he set his hand to
accomplish. He had by now become a million-
aire. He used his gift of administration as an
entrepreneur, to form several enterprises. He
owned the Southern Kitchen Restaurant in Los,
Angeles and was a backing partner in the Sub-
rena Booking Agency, the largest gospel booking agency at the time. He founded his own
company in 1985, King James Records, and
distributed a few recordings through Sound of

Gospel Records before it closed in 1990.

Gifts of Exhortation and Helps

The financial security that James Cleveland enjoyed in later years enabled him to travel extensively—both locally and abroad. He performed in humble surroundings as well as in royal residences. Cleveland and the Southern California Community Choir, along with other gospel greats that included Shirley Caesar and Andrea Crouch, appeared at Sultan's Pool Amphitheatre in Jerusalem. The concert was a huge success. Jewish people in the Holy Land shouted and danced to the music (*Ebony*, December 1983, 37). Concerts were also held in Paris, France. That experience resulted in an invitation by Prince Rainier to perform in Monaco.

Despite his personal success, Cleveland also fought to increase the recognition of gospel music at the Grammy Awards and lobbied constantly on behalf of gospel music and artists. His chief goal was to elevate the perception of gospel music ministry within the industry. Cleveland believed strongly in building up the members of the church body—specifically in the gospel music ministry. He extended the gospel heritage to a Spanish-American Pentecostal, Gene Viale, who was featured on one of his albums, to show unity in the gospel across ethnic barriers (Heilbut 1985). For all of these efforts, he was inducted into the Hall of Fame for the Gospel Music Association and The Recording Academy in 1984.

The words from *Harper's Study Bible RSV 1954* speak to these actions in 1 Peter 4: 8-11a. :

"Above all hold unfailing your love for one another, since loves covers a multitude of sins. Practice hospitality... As each receives a gift, employ it for one another... Whoever renders services, as one who renders it by the strength which God supplies ."

Rev. James A. Cleveland, the "Crown Prince of Gospel Music, " on the set of the radio program"Words to Live By.
Photo Courtesy of Getty Images.

Chapter Four:

Musical Heirs to James Cleveland in Contemporary Gospel

"Lord, let me be an instrument,
a reflection of thy love.""

—*James Cleveland, from the Grammy Award-winning*
album "Let Me Be an Instrument"

Horace Boyer (1992) asserted that the passing of the torch in gospel music ministry is akin to "apostolic succession." He explained further: "Tindley influenced Dorsey; Dorsey influenced Martin; Martin influenced Cleveland; and the genealogy goes on and on. Ten years, later, in 2002, Boyer would add "and Cleveland influenced John P. Kee (197)."

Albertina Walker, among the women of gospel, testified to being influenced by Mahalia Jackson, and, in turn, to mentoring Shirley Caesar. Thus, the heritage of African American gospel music—our black sacred music tradition—has been passed down since the period of slavery in this country from one generation to the next.

The era of contemporary gospel music was made possible in a large part by the exposure that Rev. James Cleveland gave to young songwriters. Andrae Crouch, for one, so impressed Rev. James Cleveland that Cleveland and Thurston Frazier, with whom he had started a new music publishing firm,

Frazier-Cleveland and Company, published Crouch's first song, "The Blood Will Never Lose Its Power."

Crouch bridged the gap between black and white artists with his music, and "The Blood" is now considered a standard in both black and white churches. His group Crouch and the Disciples, was multiracial, and their music a mixture of gospel and rock. In the beginning, this type of music was rejected by the black church in the same way that gospel blues had been frowned upon in previous generations. Boyer (1986) observed that:

> ...contemporary gospel is rejected by the mainstream black church, although Andrae Crouch has successfully developed a black church following [but first] after building an audience of white people, high school and college-age black students and jazz lovers (281).

Crouch is also unique in being one of the first gospel artists to deviate from the lyrics of spirituals and Professor Thomas Dorsey to devote entire songs to praise and worship, now commonly sung in Baptist, Pentecostal, and Congregational church services. Today, it is quite common to have a separate "praise and worship" service that directly precedes the start of the worship service itself.

Crouch became an ordained minister in 1990 and succeeded his father as pastor of the New Christ Memorial Church of God in Christ in San Fernando, California. In an interview with *Jet Magazine*, he revealed that he always knew he would someday pastor his father's church. His sister and co-pastor Sandra added that "It's pretty much his nature to be a shepherd because he's always had a shepherd's heart (Darden 281)."

Today, Crouch is considered to be an elder statesman of the gospel music community. He remarked in an *Ebony Magazine* interview with Walter Burrell that he now describes himself as "a minister spreading God's Word through song." He reaffirmed this belief with these words:

> God just happens to use me. I'm not His first choice, not His second, maybe not even His hundredth, but so be it. He chose me. He gave me some songs, and you just happen to hear those songs. I trust that through it all, something I write or sing will be a blessing to you (Boyer 281-282).

Forerunners of Contemporary Gospel Music

A few gospel artists were forerunners of contemporary gospel music, an industry that inherited its strength from the contributions of the pioneers who became involved in contemporary music of the 1970s and 1980s. Among those artists were Edwin Hawkins and his singers; Walter Hawkins and the Love Center Choir, the aforementioned Southern California Community Choir, Andrae Crouch and the Disciples, Sara Jordan Powell, Commissioned, Fred Hammond, Jessy Dixon, Shirley Caesar, and Billy Preston. Many of these groups were based in California. All benefitted from the legacy of James Cleveland (Fuqua 1997, 11).

Edwin Hawkins was another disciple of Rev. James Cleveland. He took the mass choir from the church to the airwaves with his recording "Oh Happy Day," which hit the charts in 1969. The song has been his greatest success to date in gospel music and led to many Grammy nominations. He, inspired by Rev. James Cleveland and Professor Thomas Dorsey before him, founded the Edwin Hawkins Music and Arts Seminar to showcase young gospel talent. The seminar is held annually in Florida. Hawkins, in speaking about the success of "Oh Happy Day," asserts that:

> I never saw the success of "Oh Happy Day" as a fluke. I've always deemed it a miracle. We were just kids with no idea in the world what we were doing. But our motives were pure – to give glory to God. We did – and He did the rest (Darden 276).

Hawkins, in advice that he gives to aspiring artists, tells them that gospel music ministry is more than an economic pursuit:

> Gospel music implies ministry, and going into the gospel music business to make money and to gain popularity is the wrong motive. The job of the gospel artist is to reach and minister to the heart and soul of man (Hampton, Score Magazine; Jan/Feb. 1993, 13).

Late Twentieth-Century Gospel Artists

The late twentieth-century gospel artists perform in what the church considers "nontraditional" venues. These "crossover" artists have been known to use the gift of evangelism in their ministry as did gospel artists of the historical and modern gospel periods. Many of these artists have participated in the Gospel Music Workshop of America, Inc. during their youth.

Groups and individuals that gained prominence during the 1980s and the 1990s include: Angie and Debbie, Yolanda Adams, Vanessa Bell Armstrong, [Kurt Carr], The Clark Sisters, Commissioned, Kirk Franklin and the Family, God's Property, Fred Hammond and Radicals for Christ, John P. Kee, Pastor Donnie McClurkin, Dottie Peoples, Marvin Sapp, Take Six, Hezekiah Walker, Be Be and Ce Ce Winans, and The Winans (Fuqua 11-12). The gospel music field is so diverse now that artists use professional networks and agents to help them break into music markets.

Kirk Franklin is another highly successful protégé of James Cleveland and also an ordained minister. Franklin says that at no time did he want to come across as the "New Messiah":

> This isn't about me. I try to represent Jesus. The power is not in the messenger, it's in the Message. For anybody who wants to do this Christian thing for real, it's a hard job, whether or not you're in the public eye (Boyer, 320).

John P. Kee is another gospel superstar that was nurtured by the legacy of Rev. James Cleveland. He was a member in the Youth Division of GMWA and also featured on two albums by the GMWA Mass Choir while still a relatively unknown artist. He returned to

GMWA to produce a "Live in Orlando" GMWA, Inc Workshop CD in 2007. The GMWA official website states "he is the only songwriter who has come back and offered his support." He brought his ensemble, the New Life Crew, and a former Youth Division board member Garland "Meechie" Waller, to work with him on the week-long project.

Franklin (1992) reminds people that it is important to realize that "black preaching and black gospel music should not be thought of in terms of a form of entertainment, but every effort should be made to understand these categories in terms of their relationship to the salvific process. He stressed the importance of understanding the "theology of history," which is the sacred oral tradition of black music. "The black music tradition must always reflect a sense of history and destiny," he maintains (123)."

Glenn Hinson in his book *Fire in My Bones: Transcendence and the Holy Spirit in African American Gospel* echoes Franklin's thoughts. He writes:

> The spiritual gift of discernment is present in gospel music. The singer, announcer, or praise leader knows when the "Spirit of God" is moving. The "gift of discernment," the mystical endowment that allows select believers to distinguish between inspired and uninspired behavior, helps believers not to become deceived. It guides them to see whether emotional excitement is holiness or show (Hinson 172).

Singing allows the singer to share the blessings of God through the anointing of the Holy Spirit. Singing has the power of touch – the power of your anointing to stir the emotions for good or for evil. Singing can condemn or redeem. Singers must sing with "spiritual intent." This way they can minister to the soul. The anointing doesn't depend on training or vocal command. The anointing allows the singer to be a vessel through which the power of the Holy Spirit is released to help another become "delivered by the power of God" (Hinson 210-212).

The Dilemma of Today's Gospel Artists

Gospel music today faces a dilemma. In its crossover appeal, it risks losing the sacredness that is its wellspring. The current controversy in contemporary gospel music was addressed in *Ebony Magazine* July 2002: "According to the new prophets, gospel is becoming a universal language, reaching not only the secular, but also the traditional community."

Guardians of gospel music's legacy maintain that it must never sacrifice its primary purpose—that of praise and worship to God. Music brings repentance. It allows the listener to see situations in the spiritual and not in the natural or physical realm. Those who hear and experience gospel music as entertainment see it through the lens of the natural—experiencing emotion but not salvation, while those who hear and experience gospel as praise and worship see it through the lens of the Spirit, feeling the outpouring of God's Spirit through song.

Gospel music facilitates our connection with our spirituality. It allows us to withdraw to a place where we can commune with God, both publicly and privately in spirit. The ministry of gospel music evangelizes the listener, i.e., prepares him or her to receive the message of the Gospel, to experience the gospel message in song.

The Secularization of Gospel Music. Gospel music no longer falls within the sole domain of the corporate church, and therein lies the dilemma. Some within the church fear that it has become too secular. After all, it is performed at jazz fests, gospel fests, country music gatherings, in night clubs, at skating rinks, casinos, and many other venues outside of the established church setting. Those settings may not present gospel music for a theocentric experience, witness, or worship (Noble 1986).

The National Football League has sanctioned gospel music fests at the Super Bowl since 1999 (www.superbowlgospel.com). A blog originally started by filmmakers and video creators features several clips of the various Super Bowl NFL Gospel Choirs. One of these clips features Gwen Belton of CBS 4 News interviewing players who participated in the 10th annual Super Bowl Gospel Fest. The Gospel Fest Choir is composed of approximately 40 NFL players.

Gospel music has even come to theme parks. Disneyworld in Anaheim, California, held its second annual "Celebrate Gospel" in conjunction with Black History Month, featuring a children's choir from the community in 2011. Corporations, also, have now become involved in gospel music by sponsoring gospel choir music competitions. Verizon, the telecommunications giant, sponsors an annual competition, "How Sweet the Sound" in which church choirs compete for the top prize of $25,000.

Gospel as Praise and Thanksgiving. Many make a distinction between commercial "ticketed" performances and performances for which musicians either accept free will, or "love" offerings, or do not expect to be paid for their musical services. The emphasis there is within the subjective knowledge domain, in one's personal relationship with God. Kemp (1983) developed a knowledge construct to show how people perceive reality. Objective perception can be measured quantitatively, while subjective knowledge is intuitive and unquantifiable by scientific means. Our spiritual heritage belongs to the subjective knowledge domain.

Gospel singers must acknowledge God's presence at all times through their delivery of the music. They do not perform for praise, self-aggrandizement, popularity, or fame. They perform in praise and thanksgiving to God for His gifts, talents, and blessings to His children. For those who are rooted in the Spirit, this poses no problem. The conflict arises for those whose music falls largely within the realm of the secular or objective domain. Often the reality of unpaid bills and financial obligations guides their actions more than worship and praise to God. Gospel music is their paycheck. The

well-being of family and one's personal in-
come are powerful forces in shaping their
motives and delivery. All too often, their
performance lacks spontaneity and is affected, designed to bring them recognition from
the audiences who buy their music and attend their concerts.

Guardians of the Art Form. The challenge
of the 21st century for gospel music ministry is twofold. Will these artists keep gospel
music as a sacred tradition, or will it become
merely a commercial form of entertainment
for one's livelihood? African American gospel singers must view their spiritual heritage
through two lenses: the politics and reality
of the objective domain must be integrated
with the subjective, intuitive heritage of
Black musical traditions. African American
gospel artists must perceive themselves as
the guardians of our sacred art form. They
must always remember our inheritance, the
legacy of our ancestors, and those who paved
the way for future generations of our music.

A Half Billion-Dollar Industry

Gospel music became big business in the ten
years following the death of Rev. James Cleveland. According to *Ebony Magazine* (July,
2002), it is the fastest growing musical genre,
and has skyrocketed from $180,000,000 in
the 1980s to a one-half billion-dollar industry at the beginning of the 21st century. The
contemporary generation of musicians and
singers, using all of the instruments associated with other music genres, took gospel to
another level with the advent of the contem-

porary gospel era. The music innovations in
the new gospel music combined elements of
rock and pop style rhythms and melodies
in the music (Peretti 2009, 146). The gospel
music industry, despite the wealth that it cre-
ates, isn't controlled by African Americans—
the very ones that generate those profits.

Promoters and music record companies
view gospel music as a production. Studios
record gospel artists for fixed rates determined by the contracts made with the record companies. This practice precludes
the artists, in many instances, from earning
substantial royalties for their work. African
American gospel artists, moreover, have not
been successful at establishing gospel music
enterprises in the manner that secular pro-
ducer/directors such as Spike Lee or Tyler
Perry have done in Hollywood. Daryl Coley
shared this insight in a 1995 *Ebony Magazine*
interview:

> If we really look at history in every
> culture, anywhere the Anglo-Saxon
> man shows up, the first thing he tries
> to do is eradicate the history and
> culture of the people, adapt to that
> genre and then turn around and say,
> "Look at what I have created," which
> is what they did with jazz and blue.
> We need to stop looking for other
> people to validate the things that
> God has given us and not allow it to
> be prostituted or given up... When I
> sing; I'm not just singing about Da-
> ryl's experience. I'm singing from

the experiences of my ancestors and what they've gone through... It's very difficult for you (Caucasians) to come from the experience of (gospel) like we do as a race of people (*Ebony* July 1995, 32).

Kirk Franklin offered this perspective in the same *Ebony Magazine* article: "We've got to control what we make. We need to control our own music because it comes from our soul (34)." There are numerous career opportunities available for African Americans in the gospel music industry of the 21st century. It is the responsibility of those within the gospel music field to become trailblazers and pioneers in [African American] non-traditional gospel careers.

The gospel music industry encompasses a number of areas beyond singing and performing. They include A & R (Artist and Repertoire) executives, music journalists, engineers, producers, promoters, distributors, agents, cover art designers, and marketers. Some of the more lucrative careers are in music business law and licensing. Advances in technology, Internet social networks, YouTube, RSS feeds, and blogs make information available instantaneously. Today's gospel artist's career must include a working knowledge of copyrights and international law for that person's optimum success and exposure. This knowledge is vital to the artist in receiving a fair share of profits from distribution of music in the international and cyberspace markets.

Music Awards and Organizations

Today, five major music awards and organizations honor gospel musicians each year. Two of them recognize Southern gospel music specifically: the Southern Gospel Music Association and the National Quartet Convention, both held in conjunction with the Southern Gospel Music Association. One of the five that bestows awards—the Country Gospel Music Association –recognizes country gospel singing.

The most coveted awards for African American gospel singers are the Grammy, awarded by The National Academy of Recording Arts and Sciences, Inc. (NARAS); the Dove Award, bestowed by The Gospel Music Association (GMA); and the Stellar Awards, created by Don Jackson, founder of Central City Productions, to recognize excellence among black artists in the gospel music industry.

The Grammy. The National Academy of Recording Arts and Sciences, Inc., is the organization that awards the Grammy, the best-known award in music. It is one of recorded music's most coveted awards, and NARAS boasts a membership of about 18,000. It recognizes and honors peers in the music industry for their artistic excellence and/or technical achievement. The awards are based on the votes of its peers within the membership of The Recording Academy.

Grammys are based on artistic achievement in all areas related to the recording industry and celebrate all genres of music. To recognize the achievements of Latino artists in the United States and Caribbean, a Latin Recording Academy was established in 1997.

Award categories include Best Recording and Performing Artist; Best Traditional and Contemporary Artist, Best Gospel, Religious, Sacred, Soul Gospel, and Inspirational Artist; Best Male and Female Vocalist; Best Choir/Chorus; Best Rock Gospel; Best Pop/Contemporary, and Best Southern or Country Artist (Gospel Music Association, 1997).

The best known gospel song of all time, "Precious Lord," in what has been a perceived a slight by the "established" gospel music ministry, has yet to be voted into the National Academy of Recording Arts and Sciences Hall of Fame. *The Dove Awards.* The Gospel Music Association (GMA) is an umbrella group that brings together all who are involved in the gospel music industry: artists, industry leaders, retail stores, radio stations, concert promoters, distributors, and local churches. The association was founded in 1964 "for the purpose of supporting, encouraging, and promoting the development of all forms of gospel music" and has more than 5,000 members (Gospel Music Association, 1997). The Academy of Gospel Music Arts, sponsored by the Gospel Music Association, is a two-day educational seminar taught by music industry professionals (Gospel Music Association, 1995).

The GMA created the Dove Awards in 1967 to recognize the growth of gospel music within the increasing diversity of Christian music. It honors outstanding achievements in Christian music, including gospel. This was due in large part to the lobbying of Rev. James Cleveland and Ed Smith to elevate the status of gospel music within the music industry.

Existing categories within the GMA are divided by racial designations. For example, the Southern Gospel category is designated for white artists, while the Contemporary and Traditional Gospel categories are for black artists. Other categories include descriptions for Urban, Country, Rock, Metal/Hard Rock, Rap/Hip-Hop, Alternative/Modern Rock, Instrumental, Choral, Children, and Musical.

The GMA's Dove Awards also recognize choral collections, special event albums, short and long forms of music, videos, album jacket designs, cover art, and graphic layout and design. There are even categories for TV programs and other media as well as awards for the D.J. of the Year and best album by a secular artist. The GMA hosts an annual "Gospel Music Week" that culminates with the awards. This presentation is televised nationally to showcase gospel music and honor the achievement of excellence in Christian music (Gospel Music Association, 1997).

The award generated controversy in 1995 when its top honor for best contribution to Black Gospel was not awarded to a black person, but to an Italian male and Latino wife team (*Ebony Magazine*, 1995, 30). Gospel musicians were outraged. African Americans felt that if the award specified an honoree by ethnicity, then the award should have gone to a person of that ethnicity. Black gospel singers contended that the Dove Award could no longer credibly showcase an ethnic group as a distinct category in the future if a member of that group was denied the honor. This sentiment was fueled by the knowledge that Rev. James Cleveland had collaborated with the GMA, for the sole purpose of creating a category to recognize African American gospel musicians.

The Stellar Awards. The Stellar Awards originated in 1985 and debuted at the Arie Crown Theater in Chicago. They honor gospel music artists, writers, and other industry professionals. The latter category was added in 2000. The Stellar Awards are notable for having special award categories for the "father "and "prince" of gospel music. The former, the Thomas Dorsey Most Notable Achievement Award, is named after Dr. Thomas A. Dorsey, "The Father of Gospel Music." The latter is the James Cleveland Lifetime Achievement Award, granted in honor of Rev. James Cleveland, popularly known as "The Prince of Gospel Music." Other annual award categories include: Artist, Song, Female and Male Vocalist, Choir, CD, New Artist, Producer, Group/Duo, Children's Performance, Music Video, Rap/Hip-Hop Gospel CD, and fan favorites for the categories of New Artist, Choir of the Year, and Song of the Year. This awards program is syndicated and viewed over major television networks.

The Future of Gospel Music: Ministry or Industry?

Gospel music has changed tremendously in its 90-year history from the late 1920s. The genre has expanded to include new forms of expression in hip-hop and rap—music that is sometimes shunned in traditional churches in the same way the gospel blues of the 1920s was unacceptable to the traditional black churches of the North.

Lisa Collins, in her book *The Gospel Music Industry Round-Up* (2009, 15), has classified gospel music into eight broad categories:

- Traditional Gospel: Participatory music designed specifically for the Sunday morning church worship experience, lyrically denoting the message of Jesus Christ
- Contemporary Gospel: "Good News" music utilizing secular influences but designed for worship both within and beyond the walls of the traditional church
- Urban Contemporary Gospel: Music incorporating street beats and urban influences; urban contemporary gospel may have a place in our spiritual lives, but not in the traditional church worship service
- Contemporary Christian: Pop-influenced Christian music
- Inspirational: Songs that are spiritually uplifting but don't necessarily convey the gospel of Jesus Christ
- New Traditional: Gospel music utilizing today's technology for its updated rhythms but rooted in the vocal and lyrical execution of traditional gospel music
- Praise and Worship: Participatory "call and response" music designed to provide worshippers with a mechanism for praise within the church experience
- Holy Hip Hop: Gospel rap-styled music

It is to be noted that gospel rap is gaining

credibility in mainstream churches because it has become a means of bringing the younger generation back to the traditional church.

Dr. Margaret Douroux, a gifted teacher, songwriter, and music director, is concerned about the future of gospel music ministry. She doesn't know, how the popularity of these new sub-genres will affect the survival of the spirit of traditional gospel music.

In an interview with the author in 2009, Dr. Douroux said: "The purpose of music ministry is to bring people to Christ. Contemporary music doesn't often have the stream that leads to Jesus. The blood is gone." She admonished today's contemporary artists: "If it doesn't lead to Jesus, don't go there. Your obligation is to lead to Jesus." Salvation, in her words, should be the primary goal of music ministry.

In a 2010 interview, Rev. Sam Roberson, former radio broadcaster, current radio advisory member, and pastor of Community Baptist Church in Henderson, Nevada, addressed a similar concern. He remarked that churches struggle with the balance of old school, new school, and hip-hop. He said that he sometimes craves the old music, but he knows that the new music has its purpose: "once you bring them to church, you must have a message."

Challenges for Today's Gospel Artists

Today's gospel artists face myriad challenges, but the most pressing ones have to do with the way they relate to gospel music as both a means of providing a living and a means of expressing their religious convictions. The

purpose of spiritual gifts, after all, is the edification of the body of Christ. The purpose
of gospel music—as a ministry and an industry—is to glorify God, edify, and entertain,
all at the same time—a tall order for an art
form. Fortunately, most of today's gospel
artists are well aware of their gospel heritage
and the songs that came before them.

The Continuing Evolution of Gospel Music

Gospel music has evolved from the days of
the early pioneers during the 1930s through
the 1960s. Sallie Martin is arguably recognized as the singer most responsible for elevating gospel to worldwide acceptance by
her work in forming choirs and choruses
through her singing tours during the 1930s
in conjunction with her work with Professor
Thomas A. Dorsey. Rev. James Cleveland referred to her as the one who "blazed the trail
for gospel music when it wasn't a popular
art form (*Ebony Magazine* March 1986, 78).

Resources and opportunities were lim-
ited during the early years of gospel music
for gospel singers such as Mahalia Jackson,
Albertina Walker and the Caravans—and
even James Cleveland and Shirley Caesar.
They received no royalties. Their concert
tours were not promoted. They didn't have
soundtracks and studio musicians to back
them as they cut records. Moreover, they experienced discrimination and segregation in
their travels across the country. Often, they
were forced to perform without pay when
shady promoters ran off with their profits.
Despite such odds, the gospel music heri-

tage of African Americans became firmly established through the life and music of Professor Thomas A. Dorsey and the Rev. James Cleveland. Rev. Cleveland, in particular, through the Gospel Music Workshop of America, worked zealously to raise the profile of gospel music throughout the world during his later years. This uniquely American form of music is recognized for its energy and its transcendence of race, denomination, affiliation, faith, and geography (DuPree and DuPree, 1993).

We in gospel music ministry and industry must retain the legacy of a people whose collective psyche preserved the musical DNA of their cultural heritage. It has survived European domination and repression. It exists from the experiences of our ancestors in Africa, Egypt and Israel. This heritage is the sum of our experiences and consciousness—our knowledge as a people. This is our legacy to the future. Our faith in God, our exercise of our gifts and talents, our witnessing of God's grace and salvation –are all important to the spread of the gospel: preached, sung, or performed. How will the 21st century gospel songwriters, musicians, soloists, and groups be remembered as the keepers of our spiritual heritage and legacy? What will their legacy be to future generations? These are questions that they must ask themselves.

PART TWO

The Gospel Music Workshop of America and Interviews with Gospel Music Griots

The Gospel Music Workshop of America, Inc. is Rev. James Cleveland's lasting legacy to the ministry of gospel music in America. Since its founding in Detroit in 1967, it has done more than any organization to elevate gospel music to its current stature as both a calling and a ministry. Moreover, it has contributed mightily in transforming gospel music into a uniquely American musical genre that has won a worldwide following.

In Chapter Five of this book, the author traces the GMWA from its humble origins as the brainchild of Rev. Cleveland to the twenty-first century contemporary music scene and describes the key features of the Workshop and the individuals responsible for making it the preeminent gospel music training ground. In Chapter Six, the author interviews pioneers and trailblazers in the gospel music field both from within the GMWA and from without: particularly from the acknowledged "Mecca" of gospel music – the City of Chicago. The interviewees shared their past experiences in gospel music ministry, their perceptions and opinions of the changes in the industry dating from the era of Professor Thomas A. Dorsey to the contemporary gospel music scene, and expressed their hopes and dreams for the future of the genre.

Chapter Five:

James Cleveland's Legacy: The GMWA

We are only God's servants... Each of us did the work the Lord gave us....What's important is that God makes the seed grow.[8] The one who plants and the one who waters work together with the same purpose....[9] For we are both God's workers. And you are God's field. You are God's building.
—1 Corinthians 3: 5-9 (NLT)

The legacy of gospel music in America is far reaching. It extends all the way from pre-slavery Africa to the struggle and oppression in America as documented by the slave songs, to the American folk music created by our enslaved ancestors, to the hymns adapted from European church worship, to the Negro Spiritual. It derives from the "bush harbor," the ring shouts, and the evangelistic campaigns that began in the late eighteenth century. Gospel music also emanates from the "gospel blues" of the "Father of Gospel Music," Professor Thomas A. Dorsey, and early pioneers of the twentieth century who endured conditions of segregation and little or no compensation or recognition to perform and sing gospel throughout this country. It continues from the "Golden Gospel Era" of the 1940s and 1950s after early pioneers and ensembles paved the way for its acceptance in churches, on the airwaves, in concert venues, in theatrical productions, and on television.

Rev. James A. Cleveland envisioned building an organization that would ensure that this vital music would continue to be presented, sung, and appreciated. His desire took shape to form the Gospel Music Workshop of America, Inc. This new organization allowed members to use their gifts and talents in music ministry in a new platform.

Indeed, the Gospel Music Workshop of America is the result of a prophetic gift given to Rev. James Cleveland to organize and inspire a group of talented individuals endowed with God-given gifts and talents to create a vehicle for young people to learn the history of Gospel music. Until that time, no forum existed for young people to sit at the feet of the masters—accomplished musicians, singers, and writers—to learn from them the skills and knowledge needed to share the gift of Gospel music. No organizational gospel bridge existed between gospel music producers and the many talented musicians who wanted to perform gospel music in venues other than the established church. GMWA was born into a time such as this, to fulfill a need in Gospel music that would provide a way for gospel ministry to reach people around the world.

The Seeds of the GMWA

James Cleveland took the training he had received as a youth under the "Master," Professor Dorsey, and leveraged his numerous contacts within the gospel music industry to advance the idea of his dream. He traveled the country enlisting the help of music promoters and singers. His vision that Chicago be the headquarters for his dream was opposed by some leaders in Chicago's religious community. He was undeterred, however, and drew up plans for the convention at its first planning meeting March, 1967, in Detroit (Personal Interview, James Ford, March 2010).

Attendees of that March meeting were: William Bryant – Dallas, Texas; James Ford – Philadelphia, Pennsylvania; Ralph Goodpasteur – Chicago, Illinois; Ronnie Ingram – Cambridge, Massachusetts; Edgar O'Neal— St. Louis, Missouri; Earl Preston – Cleveland, Ohio; Lawrence Roberts – Nutley, New Jersey; William C. Sims – Cleveland, Ohio; and Harold Smith – Detroit, Michigan (Reese, 2nd Rev. 2009, 10). Harold Smith was elected to be the first president of the organization while Rev. James Cleveland funded the new organization from his personal finances. To have a say in how the organization would be run, James Cleveland eventually took full leadership and control, assuming the presidency in 1970 (Reese, 2009, 12). He held the position until his death in 1991(Personal Interview, James Ford, 2010). The first convention of the Gospel Music Workshop of America, Inc was held at King Solomon M.B. Church and Masonic Lodge of Detroit from August 10 through August 16, 1968.

"Where Everybody Is Somebody"

Over the years, the Gospel Music Workshop of America, Inc., has chosen themes for its annual conventions that speak to the purpose of gospel music in the words of what is termed "The Great Commission" (Matthew 28:16-20). The "grace gifts" of the Spirit empower members of the Workshop to sing the gospel and use their special gifts in doing the work of the Kingdom as discerned by God's Word and His purpose for their lives. The major emphasis of each convention embodied in the national theme "Where Everybody Is Somebody," is on the equality of all members. Each person is needed, and all talents and gifts are to be used for God's glory and to minister to God's people.

GMWA, Inc. is a place where gospel music is composed, sung, taught, and performed, and where listeners receive the Gospel message in song. God's presence enables the performer, soloist, group, chorus, choir, group, quartet and the listener to connect with His power and the anointing of the Holy Spirit. Such a powerful experience frees up one's gift and allows it to operate and change lives.

The gospel is preached primarily in spiritual songs, whether they are arrangements of gospel hymns, spirituals, psalms, contemporary gospel, traditional gospel, or gospel rap. It is also a setting that facilitates spiritual renewal. These opportunities occur in nightly musicals, music seminars, and divisional activities.

The Call of Evangelism
The call of evangelism is extended throughout the annual convention. It begins with the opening communion and consecration service and continues through the daily preaching and teaching service. It is not un-

usual for an attendee to accept salvation for the first time after exposure to the myriad opportunities afforded through the Workshop's music and dance presentations. The Workshop classes end with the Friday morning commencement and closing ceremony. The Friday night musical marks the end of the shared worship experience through song with selections from the Youth Division, Men of Praise, Women of Worship, and the GMWA Mass Choir. Delegates might also hear selections from Chapter choirs to close out the convention's activities. Delegates return to their homes weary in body but renewed in spirit to minister to the needs of fellow members of the body of Christ.

Participants share their experiences at the Workshop freely through interviews and recollections. The interviewees have participated in GMWA for more than 30 years. Their stories add richness to the history of GMWA that is invaluable.

GMWA's Early Leadership

The historical developments of GMWA from its inception have been recorded in Charles F. Reese's books. Dean of the Academic Division of GMWA, his works provide the chronology of the organization and its expansion. The dates and places of board and annual convention sites provide information on the addition of programs, refinements within the constitution, and changes within the organization.

The academic division of GMWA offers the class F-Foundations 826 facilitated by Eugene Morgan that traces the historical foundations of GMWA, Inc. Mr. Morgan has taught in the Academic Division for 20 years. He has been a part of GMWA for 40 years. Members of the board and original members of GMWA participate in daily forums sharing personal stories about the organization and its growth.

Norma Jean Pender, for example, was the public relations director of GMWA at its inception, and would promote GMWA wherever she went, inviting gospel musicians and singers to join the Workshop. An associate pastor at New Jerusalem Temple Baptist Church in Detroit, Rev. Pender, is also a gospel radio announcer. James Cleveland relied on her talents greatly to foster interest and commitment to the workshop.

Ed Smith, GMWA business manager, is another person who traveled the country urging interested musicians to start chapters and become involved in this new organization. He and his wife, Sheila, during the early years of the organization, managed the business of GMWA from their flower shop in Detroit. His business acumen was indispensible to the success of GMWA.

Rev. Sam Roberson of Henderson, Nevada, recalled meeting Smith in 1975. Roberson, a radio announcer for 30 years, was recruited by Ed Smith to help establish the Silver State Chapter in Las Vegas.

Sam Roberson later became involved in GMWA as a member of the Gospel Announcers Guild (GAG) and as a Chapter Representative. He spoke of the networking within the GAG division. GAG members supported and respected each other. They used that network in whatever towns they visited. Sam Roberson spoke of the love, honor and respect shown for James Cleveland by those in the organization. He attributed this in part to how Rev. Cleveland respected the artists, singers and musicians who appeared on the nightly musicals. Rev. Cleveland demanded that the audience respect the gospel performers. A cardinal rule was that delegates remain seated or wait outside the auditorium entrance doors while the groups were performing. Disagreements that occurred backstage stayed there. Each performer was encouraged, whether he or she sang well or poorly. All were all encouraged by James Cleveland to practice their craft. Numerous gospel recording artists got their start at GMWA and have credited the organization for setting the standard of excellence and for providing exposure and opportunities for new artists.

Rev. Spencer White has ten years of experience as Nevada's chapter representative. He also mentors other chapter representatives from the more than 200 chapters of GMWA. Chapters within the United States documented by Reese (82-98) in 2007 include: Alabama, (6); Arizona (2); Arkansas (2); California (7); Colorado (2); Connecticut (1); District of Columbia(1); Delaware (1); Florida (6); Georgia (7); Illinois (3); Indiana (3); Iowa (1); Kansas (1); Kentucky (2); Louisiana (6); Missouri (3); Nebraska (1); Nevada (1); New Jersey (1); New York (5); North Carolina (5); Ohio (6); Oklahoma (2); Oregon (1); Pennsylvania (5); South Carolina (3); Tennessee (3); Texas (13); Virginia (6); Washington (1); and Wisconsin (3).

White offered this comment in speaking of the Workshop as continuing the legacy of James Cleveland: "The GMWA has the kind of music that gets down in our soul; makes you honor God and give Him thanks and glory...makes you excited – sticks with you – stirs up that inner man – something we grew up with. No one can take it away from you. The convention is uplifting. James Cleveland wrote so many songs that aren't even sung – the James Cleveland Choir sings nothing but his songs" (Personal Interview, 2010).

The James Cleveland Choir, directed by Dr. Steven Roberts, continues the legacy of Rev. Cleveland's songs. The gift of exhortation is evident in the words of Dr. Roberts, conductor of the James Cleveland Choir, and in the rehearsals of both the James Cleveland Choir and the Mass Choir. He reminded the James Cleveland Choir that "the spirit of this chorus is 100% message and ministry is the purpose - ministry is now (Rehearsal, March 2010)." Dr. Roberts is well known throughout the United States for his musical skills and talents in the musical workshop he conducts. He is also the recipient of numerous gospel awards in ten states.

Roberts also spoke of the ministry of James Cleveland and the other pioneering leaders who died within a ten-year period: Charles Nicks, Ed Smith, Donald Vails, Robert Fryson, Mary K. Elsaw, Dr. Robert Simmons, and Rev. Quincy Fielding, Sr. These members also mentored others who grew up in the organization and encouraged them to take on leadership roles. Roberts and many

others spoke of the gifts of discernment,
prophecy, and wisdom as greatly present in
the life of Rev. James Cleveland.

"He could silence the room by walking to
the piano and playing the scales of the piano
with one finger. He would minister to the
'felt needs' of the delegates, sometimes calling them specifically by their names. He also
exhibited the 'gift of helps' by the opportunities he created for unknown musicians to
become recognized. He made the careers of
many young unknown musicians and singers. James Cleveland "would stand them up
in the auditorium (2009)."

GMWA's Divisions and Auxiliaries

The divisions and auxiliaries of GMWA conduct many activities during the annual convention. Each class, worship experience,
and performance is meant to edify and build
up the members of GMWA. These divisions
and auxiliaries and their responsibilities toward the Workshop are outlined in the following paragraphs.

The Academic Division. Academic classes
are offered to enrich the spiritual lives of the
attendees. Vocal and instrumental classes
provide aspiring artists, choir members, and
musicians opportunities to learn, practice,
and grow in their respective area of talent.
The academic choral branch, the Thurston
Frazier Chorale, sings anthems and hymns at
the consecration and commencement exercises.

Scholarships, awarded in both vocal and
instrumental categories, are available to assist students in their musical endeavors.

The scholarships offered through the Academic Division include the Thurston G. Frazier Scholarship Fund, The Juanita C. Burns Scholarship Fund, and the Mary G. Gash Grant, which is restricted to faculty. GMWA offers two additional scholarships to high school students. The scholarship in Liturgical Dance was renamed in honor of Rev. Robert Simmons in 2005 (Reese 40).

Almond Dawson, a musician and arranger who lives in Chicago and was an assistant chapter representative in its early years, shared how the Juanita Burns Scholarship was instituted (Personal Interview 2009): "Mrs. Burns was married to a wealthy man. Before dying, she wanted to leave a bequest to GMWA. She shared this goal with key members of GMWA who worked with her to make it a reality. This bequest became a voice scholarship." Dr. Naomi Green of Chicago currently oversees the administration of the scholarship. The monetary value of the scholarship has increased to include more winners each year.

College credit is extended for selected courses in the academic curriculum through colleges and universities that have existing ties to the academic division. The Academic Division offers college credit through consortiums, distance learning opportunities, classes, networks, and partnerships (GMWA Official Website). The Berklee School of Music, Boston, MA, provides tuition-based financial assistance scholarships for students who attend a five-week residency summer program in music at the college. These scholarships were established in honor of Dr. Charles Fold (Reese 42).

Mobile Library. The GMWA's mobile library operates under the leadership of the Academic Division. It houses collections on the historical development of gospel music, and artifacts from various pioneers and groups. The collection was donated to GMWA by Elder William Fuqua. GMWA has a media collection of VHS and cassette tapes from the earlier years of the convention available for viewing. Visual displays include materials from individual chapters, obituaries, and souvenir program booklets from annual conventions. Information on the individual achievements of GMWA members, and the portfolio of the Chairman of the Board of Directors, Bishop Jamison, completes the collection.

The Business and Professional Guild. In striving to help individual members as much as possible, GMWA's Business and Professional's Guild charges its members within GMWA to work with the merchants and businesses in the convention's host cities.

Chapter Representatives. GMWA's chapter representatives are called "the backbone" of GMWA (Geraldine Ford Interview, 2009). Chapter representatives participate at the local, state, and national levels. They coordinate the activities of musicians at local and international chapter levels who have the interest and desire to perform gospel music and also to participate in the activities of GMWA. Chapter choirs engage in friendly competition during the nightly musicals during the convention.

The Evangelistic Board, (also known as the Ministry Division). The Evangelistic Board coordinates the GMWA's communion and consecration service. Its members provide devotional services for the week's activities upon the request of the National Board of Directors. This division also conducts an evangelistic outreach initiative in the host convention city. Moreover, the Evangelistic Board offers opportunities for delegates to attend daily prayer services within the convention setting and makes available a prayer room for delegates who desire individual prayer and intercession. Membership is restricted to clergy. Members must have approval from their pastor—through a formal letter—to participate in this ministry.

Gospel Announcers Guild (GAG). The Gospel Announcers Guild is another auxiliary of GMWA. It hosts daily programs for its members within the larger convention setting. Those discussions, panels, and presentations address marketing and distribution concerns within the music industry. Because of this single-minded focus, the GAG is not as involved in the broader goals and initiatives of the GMWA.

Says Dr. Yolanda Freeman, GAG member, co-chair of the Youth Division, and host of a gospel radio program in Chicago: "their [GAG's] schedule makes it difficult for its members to participate in other GMWA activities. GAG people have no idea of what GMWA is about, since their own services run all day long."

Men's/ Women's Councils. The men's and women's councils offer specific activities and programs for their members. The culminating activity is a musical in which the women's and men's choirs share their gifts and talents in concerts.

Nurses. GMWA nurses are on duty to assist in the medical needs of delegates and members. The GMWA provides classes for this very important function to increase the nurses' awareness and proficiency in first aid and other health-related topics.

The Performance and Recording Division. The Performance and Recording Division encompasses performance in its entirety at GMWA. It was the first division established by Rev. James Cleveland and is comprised of the James Cleveland Gospel Chorus, The National Mass Choir, and the New Music Seminar. The James Cleveland Gospel Chorus performs Rev. Cleveland's original works during the communion and consecration service and is composed of singers from throughout the country. The members come together and rehearse during board meetings and conventions for their performances of Rev. Cleveland's compositions.

The National Mass Choir is composed of 500 or more singers, musicians, and ministers of music from around the world who come together to learn songs chosen for the convention and to take music back to their places of worship. The New Music Seminar is a platform for composers and songwriters who were not selected for the National Mass Choir to have their music heard. Nightly musicals continue to be the mainstay of the convention for chapter choirs. The Division's "new talent showcases" introduce new artists.

GMWA's recording company, WEIS (Where Everybody Is Somebody), was established in 2006. Bishop Jamison and Dr. Rodena Preston are its executive director and producer. It now produces the annual convention CD.

Quartet Division. The Quartet Division performs traditional quartet music for those who enjoy this rarely performed genre of music. Classes are available for those who desire more information on this type of singing.

GMWA Security and Ushers. GMWA Security is responsible for the well-being and safety of delegates throughout the convention. Ushers assist with the needs of delegates in nightly events. They are responsible for seating and maintaining order within the performance venues.

Youth Young Adult Division. The Youth Division offers a complete program of activities that promote religious and musical training, in which GMWA's youth can develop and hone their talents. A separate schedule of classes and musicals exists for this division.

A highlight of each convention is the "Tribute to the King," a musical that recognizes and celebrates Rev. James Cleveland, the founder of GMWA, Inc. Another staple of GMWA's annual activities is the fashion show that dates to the inception of the second GMWA convention. Cotillions and "beautillions" expose youth to a Christian "debutante" experience.

The pace of the week's activities can be exhausting. With prayer and exercise beginning as early as 7:30 A.M. and the last musical sometimes ending at 2:30 A.M., it is impossible to attend all the activities of the Workshop.

"The uniqueness of the convention," says Dr. Joan Hillsman, a college professor and the Director of the Academic Division, "is its variety." She compared it to a smorgasbord—offering something for everyone" (Personal Interview, 2009). Dr. Hillsman has been active in GMWA since its inception and has instituted a "College Night," which began in 2010 and was approved to continue at the 2011 board meeting. College Night is a platform for college choirs and college musicians to perform before an audience.

The spiritual atmosphere of the convention has been known to result in healing for some delegates who are invited by ministers to reach out to fellow attendees during Daily Bread. This provides an opportunity for those present to receive Bible teaching in a corporate setting and experience a worship service with a psalmist and hear the preached gospel. Speakers are chosen by Bishop Jamison. The service offers numerous opportunities for delegates to interact with one another. In this way, GMWA embodies many characteristics of a corporate worship body. It is a place where individual members can exercise their spiritual gifts for the benefit of others, providing an atmosphere conducive to the operation of such gifts.

Gospel Music Excellence Awards Program. The Gospel Music Excellence Awards program was introduced to recognize the efforts of gospel singers, groups, musicians and instrumentalists who had achieved levels of national visibility and excellence in performance and recording in various categories of gospel music. The awards were created in response to the National Grammy Awards Selection Committee's failure to recognize all categories in the field of gospel music.

The awards were introduced at the 1982 Indianapolis Board Meeting. GMWA members fondly remember the "red carpet" award nights at annual board meetings that the award spawned. The award is no longer necessary due to the numerous opportunities for recognition in gospel music available in the secular community.

The "Yellow Book": Guidebook for the GMWA

The manual used in the original "gifting" of GMWA, and the operating manual for the organization is officially called "the Yellow Book." It makes frequent references to gifts, talents, helps, and ministering to the needs of the body. While the document lacks a publication date, it is believed to have come into being around 1974 and is accepted as the official guidebook for the operation of GMWA. The terminology used in the different editions of the publication explains how chapters and divisions evolved within GMWA. Its articles enumerate the purposes and goals of GMWA and served as a guide for the young organization during its early years.

Officers of the board in 1974 at the time the guidebook was published were:

- Rev. James Cleveland, President (Los Angeles, California)
- W.C. Sims, First Vice President (Cleveland, Ohio)

- Charles Nicks, Jr., Second Vice Président (Detroit, Michigan)
- Edward M. Smith, Executive Secretary (Detroit, Michigan)
- Robert M. Simmons, Dean (Dayton, Ohio)

Members-at-Large included: Shirley Berkeley (Washington, D.C.); Charles Craig lll (Detroit, Michigan); Charles Davis (Detroit, Michigan); Mary Elsaw (Birmingham, Alabama); James Ford (Philadelphia, Pennsylvania); J. Warren Hicks (Buffalo, New York) Al Hobbs (Indianapolis, Indiana); Albert Jamison(New York, New York); Lawrence London(Detroit, Michigan); Larry McDuffie (Savannah, Georgia); Fred Mendelssohn (Lake Worth, Florida); Charles Sanders(Chicago, Illinois); Kenneth Ulmer(Los Angeles, California); William White (St. Louis, Missouri); Isaac Whitman(Chicago, Illinois); and Tommy Williams (Buffalo, New York).

In 1988, Rev. Cleveland authorized Dr. R.M. Simmons, Academic Dean of GMWA from 1975-2000, pastor of Centenary United Methodist Church in Columbus, Ohio, and a professor of sacred music, to perform an exhaustive review and restructuring of GMWA. This needed to reflect its growth and future needs. Dr. Simmons taught *African American Music and Worship from a Historical Perspective* at Trinity Lutheran Seminary. A prolific writer, he has authored 15 books. The Board of Directors approved the revisions and a restructuring of GMWA in 1991 after the Rev. Cleveland's death.

The Vision of the GMWA 1967-1991

The 1992 revision summarized the past achievements of GMWA. It stated the purpose and objectives of the Board of Directors after the death of its founder/president – Rev. James Cleveland. The National Board of Directors focused on the following issues while recognizing a year-long mourning period:

- Who will be our new leader?
- How will we pay our bills?
- Will GMWA be able to continue and survive without our founder?

The 1992 revision outlined the changes that would take place after the official mourning period ended in March 1992. A new leadership structure was instituted, and committees were appointed to insure that the founder's vision for the Workshop continued.

The Board of Directors declared that GMWA, Inc. was fiscally sound, its operational funds were available for use, and that the Rev. Cleveland had left a financial legacy to GMWA to help ensure its survival. They assured the membership that the legacy was alive and all is well (Board of Directors statement 1992, iii).

This document therefore articulated Rev. James Cleveland's vision to upgrade the medium of gospel music. The Board of Directors acknowledged the work of those who believed in God and in GMWA's vision who were responsible for its growth and pre-eminence among gospel organizations both nationally and internationally.

The current GMWA Information Book has guided policy since the adoption of this last revision *(GMWA Information Book*, Academic Division 2001, rev. 2002, 2003). It reviews the authority exercised by the Board of Directors to make and set policy, meet each March or by special session, and create auxiliaries and standing committees. Executive Vice Chair Al Hobbs shared the revised goals and objectives of GMWA for the 21st century.

The Continuing Growth of the GMWA

The Workshop had grown from an initial planning group of 13 people in 1967 to an organization with thousands of members. Its annual conventions have filled major hotels and concert halls throughout the United States. The divisions were recognized for the work they had done as well as their enthusiasm and "gospel zeal" that gave them the impetus to act upon the vision of Rev. Cleveland. The Board of Directors confirmed its continuing goal with these words: "Those of us who remain have an obligation to continue down the path which has led this workshop to greatness (iv)." In stating the reason for the GMWA's existence, they go on to say:

In all things we give thanks and praises to God. Gospel music has been integral to the Afro-American experience....and has strengthened the power and influence of the Word of God by preparing congregations for the minister...This practice exists because the Workshop has always relied upon and operated as a vehicle for bringing lost souls to Christ. There are countless examples, in our

Workshop experience, when Rev. Cleveland would stop the song service and begin the call to salvation with literally hundreds of individuals either renewing their commitment or establishing a new relationship with God (iv).

The Board of Directors pledged that GMWA continue to spread the good news which gospel music has to offer and above all, continue to be outstanding instruments submissive to the will of a true and living God (Academic Faculty Information Guide 1991, vi)."

The Internationalization of GMWA

A historical overview added to the Guidebook's 2003 revision mapped GMWA's growth as a gospel music organization from its founding in 1967 through 2003 (Reese 2009). It includes information on programs, activities and accomplishments of GMWA. Among the noteworthy accomplishments were the:

- the creation of new international chapters
- strengthening of chapter ties
- co-teaching initiatives between members of the Academic Faculty of GMWA with members in Japan and Europe

Dr. Simmons foresaw these accomplishments that were direct results of the expansion of the GMWA. To meet the demand, he developed programs through the "African American Sacred Music Network" to address the needs of members who lived outside of the United States. The network is a consortium that provides resources in curriculum and human capital from GMWA to those in other countries. Says Dr. Simmons: "Persons from Africa, Japan, the Bahamas, France, England, Germany and other international countries were now attending convention sessions in large numbers (Reese, 30).

GMWA's Silver Anniversary

In 1992, Chicago hosted GMWA's silver anniversary at the UIC Pavilion and the Chicago Hilton Hotel. The theme was the "Dawn of a New Era." The newly elected Chairman of the Board, Al "The Bishop" Hobbs reflected on the death of Rev. Cleveland, who had brought GMWA to its present growth during its first 25 years:

> The Board of Directors has revised the constitution to meet the challenges ahead, broadened our mission and goals and recommitted ourselves to increase our service to membership development. The aim is to 'increase the penetration and acceptance of our music across the globe. All this, with the aim of seeing gospel music become the music of the world during this decade.

Ed Smith, Executive Director of GMWA, shared this reflection:

> Without a doubt, the Lord has been good to us individually and collectively. Amidst myriad challenges God has empowered us to sing songs of praise. The challenges are great,

but our commitment to significantly advance the Kingdom and continue this great work is greater. As we gather here in the Windy City of Chicago, equipping and empowering preachers, musicians, singers, directors, ministers of music, announcers, and laity to be more effective in perpetuating gospel, let's rededicate ourselves to this mission. In closing, it is my prayer that together we shall continue to advance God's Kingdom, and the beloved music of gospel.

The late Chapter Representative (2009) of the Metropolitan Chapter of GMWA, Essie Johnson Lane, expressed her gratitude to Rev. James Cleveland, Founder of the GMWA with these words: "I am grateful that Rev. James Cleveland entered into my life many years ago. His legacy will always be cherished."

"Gospeland": Cleveland's Unrealized Dream

Rev. Cleveland envisioned, as an offshoot of GMWA, the development of "Gospeland America," a national convention center that would welcome churches of all faiths. Plans for this ecumenical initiative were first conceived in 1980 and included a 350-acre complex with a facility that would have the seating capacity for 20,000 people. It was also to include an entertainment park, gospel city, temple, and amphitheatre, hotel and convention center, television and recording facilities, travel tours, auditorium and college (Reese 2004, 26-27). The dream never came to fruition, however, likely because of the ambitiousness of its scope, and Cleveland's untimely death.

Postscript: GMWA Today

The GMWA of 2011 is very different from the organization begun in 1967. The organization has chapters and delegates from the United States, the Bahamas, Canada, Denmark, England, Japan, Italy and Sweden who attend the annual convention. Today, there are more than 200 chapters and more than 28,000 members. Corporate sponsorships, university partnerships, and scholarships that did not exist during the GMWA's early years are available for today's participants. Technological advances allow musicians to learn on the latest music software, computers, keyboards, and instruments. In addition, numerous opportunities exist for personal spiritual edification, shared knowledge experiences, group fellowship, and networking during the convention.

The economic realities of the 21st century, however, pose grave questions about the operation of GMWA and the ability of its members to meet the higher costs of housing, transportation, and related convention expenses. Interviewees addressed the issue of economics related to the GMWA.

Mattie Robertson, a Thurston Frazier Chorale director and member of the Academic Faculty, said that GMWA leadership should "make it affordable for all people." Annie Bowen, who was affiliated with the James Cleveland Workshop in the 1960s echoed the same sentiment: "Streamline fees for participants," she said. Dr. Carl Bentley, associated with the GMWA since the 1970s and who was also a participant in Professor Dorsey's Nation Convention of Choirs and Choruses, lamented that "the expenses of the Work-shop currently taxes the poorer participant. Many people labored in the Workshop to make it what it is."

Other members reflected on the purpose of GMWA. A major tenet of the author is that GMWA is an organization in which gifts of the Spirit are exercised and visible. The author's interviews and with members of the Academic Faculty and the Chapter Representatives both proved and disproved that belief. A few of their responses to this belief are shared in this chapter, while other participants in gospel music ministry expounded on the issues in the next chapter in the extended interviews.

Raymond Wise, a member of the Academic Faculty who has conducted music and worship seminars for more than 23 years, grew up in GMWA and came through its Youth Division. He recalled the leadership that provided a structure with a purpose, plan, and discipline for the youth. Today, he encourages people to "shine your light in your own environment. The purpose of GMWA was not for the manifestation of spiritual gifts in the way a conference on ministry would be," he said. "Gifts within the Workshop are seen specifically – not globally." (Personal Interview 2009).

Dr. Herbert V.R.P Jones, a choral conductor and theomusicologist, is executive assistant to the dean of the Academic Division of GMWA. Dr. Jones sees many gifts of the Spirit operating in music ministry. He stated further that all of the spiritual gifts were present in the founding of GMWA. He sees the gospel message as preached, sung, and lived.

Dr. Kenneth Peterson, a member of the Academic Faculty and the Gospel Announcers Guild asserted that, "GAG incorporates all of the gifts of the Spirit – state chapters and city chapters—spreading the gospel through Word and song. An attack on Christian media is present in today's environment," he adds. "Yet the gift of discernment operates in GMWA. You can call out what's not right...there are people here [in the GMWA] who walk in the Spirit. "gospel music ministry must glorify God (Personal Interview 2009) ."

The GMWA of the 21st century faces many difficult questions. Among them:

- What can be done to make the convention more affordable?
- How can constituents be empowered in the decision-making of the National Board of Directors?
- What long-range plans exist for establishing a permanent gospel music collection?
- What aspects of "Gospeland" should and will become a reality?
- How does our present direction align with our stated vision, mission, and purpose?

Answers to these questions require soul searching at the highest levels. But it is the responsibility of those who make up the membership of GMWA, who desire to perpetuate the ministry of gospel music, and who are witnesses—through music—to the message of the gospel, to act. Proposals can be drafted within the individual chapters. Recommendations can be made to the Board of Directors and through the various divisions and auxiliaries of GMWA. Research and evaluation can be conducted through e-mail with the membership to gather information for further decision-making. In the final analysis, we the members are responsible for the future of the GMWA. It is our heritage and our legacy, and we must ensure that it is preserved for future generations.

Chapter Six:

Interviews with Gospel Music Griots

"If it had not been for the Lord on my side,
where would I be? Where would I be?
— Margaret Douroux

The author interviewed key figures in the gospel music ministry within the Gospel Music Workshop of America, Inc. and those who live in the "Mecca" of gospel music—the city of Chicago. The interviewees are pioneers and trailblazers in the gospel music industry and respected evangelists and teachers in gospel music ministry. They served in the tradition of West African griots and, through oral history, provided texture and composition to the gospel music experience in America.

They include mentors, singers, choir directors, musicians, music educators, as well as gifted songwriters whose hymns have become standards in contemporary gospel music. The author is grateful to them for generously sharing their experiences and insights about the ministry as well as their perspectives on the direction and challenges of the gospel music ministry in the twenty-first century.

Evangelist Lorraine Allen
(Personal Interview, August, 2009)

Evangelist Lorraine Allen and her husband, the late Professor Ernest Allen, trained musicians at his studio of music in Chicago for many years. She is an anointed singer and member of a Levitical family of preachers and singers. Her daughters are also singers and evangelists. She shared the following impressions about the gospel music industry in an interview with the author.

"Gospel music is both entertainment and spreading the gospel. It is considered a ministry when [members of] those in the Body of Christ minister in song. Their singing helps people to know about Jesus – their testimony helps to introduce them to the Word."

Lorraine remembers being stopped by a person who said his heart was so touched by a song that she sung years ago. His life was changed. He is now filled with the Spirit and found his ministry in singing. Evangelist Allen spoke of the difference between being talented and being anointed:

"Sometimes artists are talented without the anointment. Feeling comes from that singing in the world. Every good and perfect gift cometh from above– although it is used in the natural (world). That spirit that touches the emotions and feelings of the listener still comes from the singer's gifts."

Evangelist Allen elaborated on the subject of spiritual gifts in music ministry:

> Musicians as well as singers have spiritual gifts. The difference is how they perceive themselves. Gifts do not come just by studying music or being a child prodigy. The gifts come from God's anointing. The musician

must have a relationship with God. When that relationship changes, then their music changes. Music brings a connection, and when the Spirit is felt, there is a connection. The question is: Does the musician understand and relate that it comes from the Lord"?

The attitude of those who play instruments and sing changes the atmosphere of worship experiences. Evangelist Allen asserts that, "church services and worship experiences bring people into an atmosphere of praise. The atmosphere changes with the musicians and the Spirit that they bring to the body of Christ."

Mrs. Allen and her late husband Professor Ernest Allen perceived music from the perspective of God using their gifts for His glory. She has observed the difference when music emanates from a gift and has watched her husband draw it out of musicians under his tutelage.

"There were people who have always wanted to play music. They were brought to a point of knowing how to play gospel. Some of those students didn't know white notes from black notes," she said.

In her classes, Evangelist Allen observes her students changed by the touch of God. Some of them shed tears prompted by His anointing and by the Holy Spirit. She adds:

A person must acknowledge their gifts. A person may have a fantastic, melodious voice and all may love her professional delivery. On the

other hand, a person without that gift can tear up the church in spite of being a non-professional and having never studied music – voice croak-ing – scratchy. That doesn't stop the anointing from coming through
the appointed vessel if the person has acknowledged the Source of the gift. You must acknowledge that the Holy Spirit has used you and thank those that compliment you.

Delois Barrett-Campbell
(Personal Interview   February, 2011)

Delois Barrett-Campbell is known through-out the country and Europe as an anointed gospel singer and is recognized as one of Chicago's "Living Gospel Legends." She and her sisters, The Barrett Sisters, have sung gospel music for more than 50 years and have performed in Europe more than 30 times. Mrs. Barrett-Campbell herself has sung the gospel for more than 70 years. The people in Europe are such fans of hers that she still receives requests to return.

Mrs. Barrett-Campbell's musical career as a singer began with her first job after comple-tion of high school. Her employment with gospel great Roberta Martin lasted for about 19 years. She also joined Professor Dorsey's organization and began singing in the Youth Department of the National Convention of Gospel Choirs and Choruses. It was where she was first noticed for her musical talent.

"I Love the Name Jesus" was the first solo I sang during that convention," she recounted in an interview. "I have sung for Queen Mahalia Jackson, Sally Martin, and of course, Roberta Martin."

A huge picture of Mrs. Barrett-Campbell with the Roberta Martin Singers is featured prominently in her living room as well as one of her group, The Barrett Sisters. In the 1960s, Barrett-Campbell was one of the first gospel singers to be featured on Sid Ordower's gospel show "Jubilee Showcase" in Chicago—years before gospel was promoted in the media. She proudly recalls being asked to sing at the funeral of one of her role models, Dr. Thomas A. Dorsey.

While Barrett-Campbell was never a part of GMWA, she was nevertheless a good friend of James Cleveland, who grew up in the same gospel music environment in Chicago as she had.

"James came to my house whenever he was in Chicago," she revealed in the interview. "He loved for me to fix him pork chops and rice."

Barrett-Campbell celebrated her 85th birthday in March, 2011. Due to growths on her vocal chords, she has not been able to sing, and she misses the opportunity to sing more than anything else.

"Gospel music," says Mrs. Barrett-Campbell, "is the Word through music by grace." She has sung gospel music when singers were paid little or nothing. Her motivation was praise to God. "Gospel singers," she confided, "never get paid what they deserve."

She has lived her life to praise God. That is all she has lived for or wanted to do. She gives Him all the glory and honor. She thanks Him for the privilege of being one of His messengers.

In comparing gospel music today to the traditional gospel music that she sings, Mrs. Barrett-Campbell remarked: "Gospel music" [today] is more instrumental...the [true] message of gospel music is in the words. You know when you're singing under the anointing."

She acknowledges that her gift is a God-given talent: "I never had a voice lesson...I don't know C from D on the piano. I've given my life to God. I praise God for how He has used me. I'm not an evangelist – I'm a gospel singer," she maintains.

Mrs. Barrett-Campbell has used her gifts of exhortation and encouragement to minister in song to those in prison as well as those in the church, at gospel fests, and concert halls. She is clear, however, about her purpose. "What I do is under the anointing of God... my life is one of praise and adoration to God for the ability to lift my voice in praise to Him for His goodness." The Barrett Sisters are being recognized for their contribution to gospel music in a documentary scheduled to air in July or August 2011.

Dr. Carl Bentley
(Personal Interview, September, 2009)

Dr. Carl Bentley has been associated with GMWA since 1977. He is an artist, minister, songwriter, and pastor. He has a syndicated radio broadcast and webcast. Dr. Bentley was associated with Professor Thomas A. Dorsey's National Convention of Gospel Choirs and Choruses, where he taught and worked with the soloist's bureau. His role with the Dorsey convention was to help train singers to become soloists. The focus of soloist training has changed from the era of Thomas A. Dorsey and Willie Mae Ford Smith in that now, with the GMWA, it has become more competitive.

Dr. Bentley is a participant in the three historic gospel music organizations in existence today: The Hampton University Ministers Conference, The National Convention of Gospel Choirs and Choruses, and The Gospel Music Workshop of America. He compared the distinctions among the three entities and their impact on gospel music ministry.

> Hampton is a much older organization whose function and purpose was different from that of Professor Dorsey and Rev. Cleveland. Participants sung, anthems for the entire convention. When gospel was sung it was like a breath of fresh air.
>
> The scale of The National Convention of Gospel Choirs and Choruses is much smaller than the GMWA. While the focus is the same in that both teach and both sing, the substance is different. It is more of a ministry for choir directors, church members and choir leaders. GMWA is a "Mecca" for gospel music offering something for everyone—technology, skills—a complete how-to-do list for a gospel artist. GMWA's focus has shifted with the death of James Cleveland to one with more industry involvement.

"The genius of Rev. Cleveland," asserted Dr. Bentley, "was the combination of "emotionality with spirituality. He was able to move a Workshop audience from focusing on self and the emotions accompanied with self-absorption to focusing on God and the worship of Him for who "He is".

Dr. Bentley expressed the following thoughts about gospel music:

> Gospel is both preached and sung. When the gospel is sung, it moves the person not only to a knowledge of God, but to salvation if he or she is not saved. The sung gospel is the 'good news' of God. James Cleveland was a father figure to the younger musicians. He inspired awe. Everyone wanted to be like him. I observed 10 piano players waiting for the opportunity to play one song in a visit to his Cornerstone Institutional Baptist Church. Rev. Cleveland inspired many musicians, singers, songwriters, and composers. It was the dream of all musicians in the Workshop during the 1970s to go to California, attend Cornerstone, and become successful. This was during the early years of GMWA when many divisions of the Workshop were being developed, instituted and put in place by the founder and the board of directors.

Bentley's vision for GMWA is that of a consumer – not a leader or producer. He wants the Workshop to be just what it is: "something for everyone, yet with a greater emphasis on training young people in worship and to be servants of the church. Stardom should be minimized. "The focus should be on worshipping the Lord."

He recalls one night, in particular, when Rev. Cleveland was ministering: "God's anointing upon James Cleveland was obvious. I felt God operating in my innermost being. I was now able to see past the glitter, the power and prestige. I wanted to be like him because of his position."

Dr. Bentley wants youth to see and understand music ministry as a spiritual gift – not only as a natural talent. "Worship is serving God, recognizing God and honoring Him for who He is as described in Dr. Robert Simmons's book *Seeing the Majesty of God*," he says.

He recalled persons who were instrumental to the growth and success of GMWA. Each made each other great. "Fred Mendelssohn was in charge of Savoy records and attended GMWA. Ed Smith was the business manager who saw that all went smoothly and paid bills. These people were nurturing and mentoring to the youth – took them under their wings and encouraged them. What the youth received at the Workshop carried them through the next year – it was something they looked forward to. They would then emulate leaders such as Donald Vails and Myrna Summers, and go back home and apply the skills and lessons they learned back at their home churches."

Annie Bowen
(Personal Interview, March 2010)

Annie Bowen has a rich background in music ministry. She and her husband John Bowen, a renowned singer and musician, are very active in gospel music. Mrs. Bowen describes herself as a "background singer" while crediting her husband as the gospel music maestro. She was affiliated with the James Cleveland Workshop in the late 1960s in Chicago. Mt. Pisgah Baptist Church, where the minister of music was the famous gospel singer and recording artist Roberta Martin, was her church home.

Mrs. Bowen, a choir member, met her husband when he became the musician for Mt. Pisgah. He worked with Roberta Martin from 1959 to 1969 and succeeded her after her death in 1969. His musical ministry included working with Dorothy Sykes, Jessy Dixon, Milton Brunson, Maceo Woods, and Marvin Yancey–all well-known Chicago gospel artists. Her husband also played and arranged music for the Lucy Rodgers Singers of Chicago.

"We married at Mt. Pisgah," Mrs. Bowen stated.

She recalls the work she and her husband performed in gospel music ministry while living in Chicago: "James Cleveland, at that time, was working at the studio with Roberta Martin. The Barrett Sisters were also a part of the Chicago gospel music scene."

She also recalls Albertina Walker and the Caravans rehearsing at their home in Chicago before some of their road trips. "On one occasion, I even designed the costumes for their tour to Nevada," she said.

Mr. Bowen accepted a teaching job in Colorado Springs in 1980. The couple eventually moved to Colorado Springs. They later became involved in the choir "Unity in the Community." Subsequently, it became chartered as the GMWA Colorado Springs Chapter under the leadership of P.M. Wynn and Donna Munn. The Colorado Springs Chapter first attended a GMWA convention in 1989 in New Orleans, Louisiana. John Bowen currently serves as the musician for the chapter choir. It won awards in Denver in 2010 and 2011 for "Best Choir" in the choir competition.

"The Colorado Springs Chapter is very active," Mrs. Bowen says proudly. It participates in local events in Colorado that include annual Dr. Martin Luther King tributes and performances during the Christmas season. The chapter choir sang at the Civic Center in December 2009 and with the Colorado Springs Symphony Orchestra.

She spoke of other venues in which the Colorado Springs Chapter Choir has participated: "The choir served as background singers for such famous artists as Albertina Walker, whenever she appeared in town. Sometimes Albertina would bring a musician, and sometimes my husband John would play for her. Her last trip to Colorado was two years before her death in 2010."

Bowen and her husband most recently worked with singer Angela Spivey on her tour in Colorado. Her vision for GMWA is that it will grow in structure, faith, and materials. "More could be done to grow spiritually, show integrity, and set an example," she believes.

Concerned about the financial constraints that GMWA faces currently, she suggests that a portion of annual surplus monies be placed in high-yielding investment instruments that have the potential to return profits to GMWA. She ended the interview by reiterating that GMWA set an example, grow in love, strength, faith, and put in place a program to achieve these outcomes."

Almond Dawson
(Personal Interview, August, 2009)

Almond "Sonny" Dawson is a superb pianist and arranger who lives in Chicago. He was an assistant chapter representative for GMWA during the 1970s. He is well-known throughout the country for his work with choirs and the Inspiration Singers, a pioneering Chicago group during the 1960s and 1970s. Dawson expressed the following thoughts about spiritual gifts and their relationship to gospel music:

> The composition of songs and spiritual gifts enables you to hear a melody that you've never heard before that lies in the deep recesses of your mind. This allows you to create the words to the song. The Lord just gives it to you all together: sometimes the words, sometimes the melody. Often you'll get them both while you're sitting at the piano. One comes and then the other. To me, this is a spiritual gift.

Dawson shares his perspective on the nature of music ministry and gifts and talents:

Singers feel a call to express their talent. Many times I have written an arrangement for one particular person, but as I am writing it, another soloist comes to mind – an example of the gift of discernment. You have to know within yourself what person is to sing a particular song – know that this is the right choice for a lead singer. It is the gospel set to music – not the preached or read work – but it can be set to music.

The subject turned to Thurston Frazier, one of the persons who was instrumental during the GMWA's formative years. Frazier was a classically trained musician and a proficient reader [of music] who inspired James Cleveland to delegate to him the task of developing the more sacred part of the Workshop by forming the Workshop's chorale. The group's charge was to sing sacred music, some of which was composed by the academic faculty. Rev. Cleveland invited alumni who could read music to become a part of the chorale. Out of respect to Thurston Frazier, the Academic Chorale, was renamed the Thurston Frazier Chorale after his death.

Dawson recalled that Thurston Frazier was a fantastic musician who read music: "Part of the Workshop's goal was to [create] music at all levels and [develop] musicians who were capable of answering the call for whatever music was needed." In describing the role of the church choir, Dawson says: "It prepares the way through music for the congregation to accept the preached Word."

Almond Dawson, as does Evangelist Lorraine Allen, describes the difference in singing under the anointing from singing with a talent or skill. "When singers sing in the world, their gifts come through when they get lost in the words. You [sense] the difference in a performance, and [you know] when it's real. The listener knows when the person gets caught up."

Dawson speaks of the changes in the GMWA convention over the years. He acknowledges that in offering something for everyone, the variety of choices can be overwhelming to the new delegate. He reflected that the convention was very spiritual when James Cleveland was alive and feels that is what needs to be recaptured: "At the end of the convention on Friday nights, James would sing 'Until He Comes Again' as attendees hugged, cried, and said good-bye to each other. Friday should end on a high spiritual note – that is missing."

Concerning the gifts and talents of Rev. James Cleveland, Dawson says: "He had a very unique feel for music...for his arrangements and for the beat...James Cleveland was uniquely qualified to feel the beat."

Dawson concluded with his vision for the future of GMWA. He would like to see support for a permanent location for the convention, where its gospel music collection might be displayed at a permanent exhibit. Detroit, Michigan, the birthplace of GMWA, would be a suitable location for a gospel music museum, he feels. "This organization has been in existence for almost 45 years. We need something to show for that," he says.

Dr. Margaret Douroux
(Personal Interview, July 2009)

Dr. Margaret Pleasant Douroux has been a catalyst in music ministry throughout her life and is an inspiration for those in the Workshop and music ministry. Dr. Douroux, a renowned member of the Academic Faculty, teaches about the importance of music ministry in her classes. She also provides training through her foundation to further develop the presentation of Sunday morning worship music. She selects and uses music in all parts of her ministry to highlight who Jesus is.

Her music has been published in hymnbooks, sung worldwide at Resurrection services, and printed in church bulletins as an integral part of worship services. All of her songs are grounded in Scripture and are high expressions of praise and reverence to God. Two of her best known songs, "Give Me a Clean Heart," and "I'm Glad" were introduced to GMWA before she became affiliated with the Workshop in the 1970s.

A gifted teacher, composer, music director, minister of music, music publisher and lecturer, Dr. Douroux conducts workshops throughout the nation and has received numerous awards and honors. Dr. Douroux freely shares her God-given spiritual gifts. She founded the Heritage Music Foundation in California, which hosted its 25th annual gospel music conferences in 2010. Her lifelong goal is to establish Gospel House, dedicated to preserving the heritage and legacy of gospel music.

The primacy of morning worship is the focus of her ministry, and the choir's responsibility in music ministry is of paramount importance for the worship experience. Dr. Douroux and Dr. Steven Roberts (whose interview appears later in this chapter) received the Alma Hendricks Award in 1992. The award recognizes songwriters whose songs have been recorded by the GMWA Mass Choir. The following are Dr. Douroux's thoughts on the subject of the direction of contemporary gospel music:

> Bringing people to Christ—En Garde—says that there is a need to discern the direction in which our music takes the congregation. Is it leading to Christ, or is it [sending] a mixed message? Some want hip-hop in the church because it is a draw for the kids. Some people sing music that they think will [bring down] the house; that is, they address the audience as if it is entertainment. A competitive attitude has developed since the [Bakker's] PTL (Praise the Lord) [of the 1980s] and the stations and networks have brought new talent to TV. Now, church people mimic what they see on TV – bringing into the church – entertainment – not worship. Contemporary music often doesn't [serve as] the stream that leads to Jesus. The blood is gone.

She shared these words of Dr. James Abbington, Associate Professor of Church Music and Worship at Candler School of Theology, Emory University. He is also Executive Director of the African American Church Music Series, and Co-director of the annual Hampton University Ministers and Musicians Conference: "They sing seven words eleven times."

On the purpose of the Sunday morning worship service, Dr. Douroux says:

> On Sunday morning what you do must lead to Jesus; otherwise, don't go there. A soloist or praise team, can't save or heal anyone. They can't heal or deliver. There's only one Source–one Star–and you ain't it. His instruction to us is often exactly the opposite of what we're doing. Ministries are now trying to get children into the church. Our job is to lift so that Jesus can draw. We've gotten so confused.

Expanding on these sentiments, Dr. Douroux adds:

> The audience doesn't have to like me in order for me to praise Him. I'm not sure where we're going or where we're going to end up. Changing the direction of our worship often goes to a place that has no essence, healing, or fulfillment. Songs like "Amazing "Grace" and "I Need You Every Hour" can't go home with us. What you've been pumped up for on Sunday is gone on Monday. Grandmother

could iron for the white boss—pour
starch on white clothes and hum. It
made us free even while we were in
bondage. I'm not sure where we're
going now.

She believes that unless the foundation is
true to God "we're sounding brass and tin-
kling cymbal."

Reflecting on her gift further, Dr. Douroux
reveals : "I almost felt guilty using my name
as a writer. 'Give Me a Clean Heart,' 'He Decided to Die,' and 'If It Had Not Been for the
Lord on My Side' are all scriptural.

She recalls one night, when she was on her
way to choir rehearsal, hearing God speak to
her. The words to "If It Had Not Been for
the Lord on My Side" came through God
ministering to her spirit. She added that she
didn't know why God gave her the lyrics to
"Give Me a Clean Heart," but she taught
the song to a mediocre young adult choir because of the newness of what God was doing in her. She had no idea that God would
use the song in a hymnbook to represent a
generation of people or to be sung around
the world. It had to be the gift of the Spirit.
The songs "Chosen," "Resting Place," and
"Trees" (drawn from the Book of Judges) are
other songs that God gave to her.

Margaret Douroux, in high school, was
discouraged from pursuing her dreams of a
college education. A high school counselor
had advised her to take shorthand and typ-
ing. She became a teacher, school counselor,
and school psychologist in Los Angeles and

later earned PhD in education. She referred to herself as a "mediocre student." Today, she stresses how important it is to stand on what has God given us. "Believe in what God speaks to your spirit," she says.On Rev. James Cleveland's spiritual gifts Dr. Douroux says:

> I think Rev. James Cleveland knew God allowed for the gifts. During the nightly musicals when he was alive the delegates would dance, pop, whip. He'd come in and sing "I am Thine," hush the group, and change its spirit. He realized that he needed the Spirit of God to bring the unity between His Spirit and what was happening in the nightly service.

Missing that spirit now, Dr. Douroux finds it hard to get beyond the pump, pump, pump of much of the contemporary music. She remembers hearing a choir sing "He Decided" during a nightly musical. "It changed the entire tone of the service," she said. Dr. Douroux is concerned about the future of gospel music ministry. She muses on the future generations, thinking of how she is raising her grandchildren. "We may have lost a generation of kids who don't know how or why we worship, but who respond to the 'beat'," she laments.

Dr. Douroux carries a great burden for this lost generation of children: "People are hungry for the Scripture. So many people express the emptiness they feel within the church. Often the spirit of invitation is competitive. The choir wants to shine and over sing at the time of invitation. But Jesus is in the competition, and I know He isn't going to fight for a space."

Geraldine Ford
(Personal Interview, August 2009)

Geraldine Ford is the wife of National Board Member, James Ford and mother of National Board Member Je Juan Ford. She was active in the National Convention of Gospel Choirs and Choruses before joining GMWA. She has worked in many capacities within GMWA, including the Youth Division and the Fashion Show. Mrs. Ford had the privilege of knowing Rev. Cleveland during his tenure with the National Convention of Gospel Choirs and Choruses and with GMWA. Moreover, he was as a frequent guest in her home due to his friendship with her husband.

"The emphasis of GMWA was always on gospel music," Mrs. Ford related in an August 2009 interview. "GMWA is unique because of its length: the number of daily activities makes it different from other conventions. Activities last from 7:00 A.M. to 2:00 A.M. The convention runs Sunday to Friday. Opportunities exist at various services during the week for persons to give their lives to Christ."

Philly Mass was the first and largest chapter for the first five years of the GMWA, and Washington, D.C. was the second largest chapter. Mrs. Ford fondly recalls the "friendly competition" between chapter choirs from the East and West Coasts under the leadership of Bishop Albert Jamison of New York and Dr. Rodena Preston of California to see which chapter would have the largest choir in attendance.

"Bishop Jamison brought Daily Bread to the convention in 1996 to help pastors understand the convention better," Mrs. Ford said. He also instituted a workshop, "Bridging the Gap" for pastors and ministers of music, which helped to change the image of the convention for many ministers, she related. These efforts brought more ministers and pastors into the convention. Says Mrs. Ford:

> There were many different reasons that ministers didn't attend the convention or promote it to their members. One was jealously. Another was the perception of the people who attended this music convention. The classes for the ministers of Music and Daily Bread helped to clarify communication between pastors and musicians. Pastors began to allow their members to become delegates.

"Nightly musicals drew larger crowds in the early years," Mrs. Ford recalled. "Attendance is not what it used to be – particularly because of the number of on-going activities. Midnight services used to begin at 12:00 A.M. and last until 2:00 or 3:00 A.M. Youth and young adults would be 'jamming in another location.'" She feels that the workshop is better because today there are more educational, spiritual, and musical opportunities available to delegates.

"The workshop has expanded tremendously since the early days," she shared. "The Academic Division is three times its original size. There are both positive and negatives to the growth of any organizations, however, as growth also requires more resources," she admits.

The Youth Division, established in 1973, has grown tremendously since then. Before it was established, youth came to the convention with their families, but there were no structured activities for them to participate in, leaving them with nothing constructive to do while their parents were busy in classes and other functions. The division was created to address this problem.

She believes that Rev. Cleveland may have asked Robert Fryson to develop the division. Both he and Yolanda Freeman worked with the youth, in addition to Eleanor Harris, Leatha Lucas, and Christine Brown who were youth division supervisors. Ford also worked with the youth. Berniece Jamison-Turner began the praise dancing and dance curriculum for the division. Due to its appeal, an adult praise ensemble was instituted. Tangie Dickson from Philadelphia and others began the adult praise ensemble, she recalled.

"Youth activities, initially, were held during the day," Mrs. Ford reminisced. "John P. Kee and Kirk Franklin, started the midnight musicals for the youth. Kee eventually left to pursue his own musical goals but returns periodically to lend his gifts and talents to the Workshop. He produced the Workshop album in Florida in 2008," she said.

Mrs. Ford identifies those who later served as leaders within that division: Minister David Allen took responsibility for the guidance of the Youth Division after the death of Robert Fryson. Craig Hayes from Trenton, New Jersey, and Sam Bennett from Buffalo, New York worked under David Allen. The Youth Division expanded into the Youth/Young Adult Division. A Youth Board of Directors (consisting of 10 members) was established by Bishop Jamison. Garland Waller (Meechie) was appointed by Bishop Jamison to serve on this board. Waller served as president in 2003-2004 (Reese 2009, 65). Craig Hayes served as vice president. Rev. Hayes now serves on the national GMWA Board of Directors. Youth advisors are listed as Minister David Allen, Ms. Christine Brown, Mr. Leroy Creighton, and Dr. Yolanda Freeman (Reese 2009, 65).

Says Mrs. Ford:

> The Youth/Young Adult Department became very popular. They had a separate convention–complete with their own space and time slots. This schedule caused dissension when some of the adult delegates stopped going to adult functions and began fraternizing with the youth. The Youth Division also had its own church service, maintained its musical instruments, and contributed money to the GMWA organization. The youth had separate concerts and albums. Their concerts were well attended and sometimes conflicted with the nightly adult musical schedule. The youth board was eventually dissolved.

Mrs. Ford then discussed the origin of the classical component within the Academic Faculty.

> Thurston Frazier was the "bigger than life" genius organ player from Detroit. He loved anthems and hymns. Rev. Cleveland asked him to add more than gospel music to the convention. In response, Frazier organized the Alumni Chorale. Its repertoire was sacred music. This added a new dimension of music to the Workshop. The Alumni Chorale, later named for Frazier, is devoted to singing sacred music: anthems and some hymns. They render selections at the communion and commencement services.

Mrs. Ford recalled Rev. Cleveland's inclination to allow the persons he chose for leadership positions to use their talents to glorify God and build up the GMWA body. She says, "Rev. James Cleveland knew people everywhere and brought people with different gifts together to form the Workshop. It flourished. Charles Sanders, an editor for *Ebony Magazine*, served on the advisory board of directors. Dr. Charles William Sims, an educator, helped to build the Academic Division. He was the first vice president of the Board of Directors for many years. In 1976 Charles William Sims was GMWA's 'head man'."

In concluding the interview, Mrs. Ford emphasized that chapters are the life-blood of the convention: "The Workshop is a platform where young artists of today can learn and possibly be discovered. They have that purpose in mind when attending the Workshop. But the chapters come for the music and the classes and are the ones who support GMWA's classes and services religiously. They are the backbone of the convention."

Mr. James Ford, Original Board Member
(Personal Interview, March 2010)

Board member James Ford is the last remaining member of the original GMWA board established in 1967. He was a personal friend of the founder Rev. James Cleveland and a well-known gospel promoter in Philadelphia, Pennsylvania. Mr. Ford also served as president of the Victory Choral Ensemble, a prominent singing group in Philadelphia and was instrumental in the formation of the Philadelphia chapter of GMWA.

Philadelphia had the first mass choir and was the first GMWA chapter formed after the board meeting in 1967 and before the first convention in 1968. Mr. Ford recalls a conversation he had with Rev. Cleveland during one of his visits to Philadelphia. Rev. Cleveland sat in his kitchen and talked about his dream of forming a gospel music association. James Cleveland often ate at his home whenever he was in Philadelphia and had many discussions on the subject.

This seed for a music workshop germinated three years before a decisive board meeting took place in Detroit at the London Inn on Woodard Street. A board of nine people was formed to help foster and promote the Cleveland Gospel Music Association. Harold Smith originally served as the first president. Lawrence Roberts was the vice president. Procedural rules of order in the first meeting prevented Rev. Cleveland from expressing ideas without following protocol. This didn't sit well with him because his resources were responsible for the formation of the organization.

The incorporation papers were later drawn to reflect James Cleveland as both founder and president in 1967. The name of the music association became the Gospel Music Workshop of America, Inc. The papers of incorporation were signed by Annette Mays-Thomas, Ed Smith, James Cleveland, and Sheila Smith. Annette Mays-Thomas and Sheila Smith became members of the board following the death of James Cleveland. The position of president was retired after Rev. Cleveland's death.

The office of chairman of the board was instituted with the election of Al Hobbs in 1992. He served from 1992 to 1996. Says Mr. Ford:

> Record companies were big when Hobbs took over. He brought corporate sponsors into the convention. The workshop was the place in the gospel music industry to become well known, to come into contact with record companies, to showcase their talents, to gain knowledge, and to enhance their musical gifts. Singers, songwriters, musicians, all came to the annual workshops. Those with existing music contracts would come but could not be taped.

Mr. Ford reminisced:

> Andrae Crouch came to Workshops.
> They all came through here: Kirk
> Franklin, Myrna Summers, and
> Yolanda Adams, John P. Kee, Keith
> Pringle, James Moore, Thomas Whit-
> field, Daryl Coley. Kurt Carr comes
> every year. He was the "Tribute to
> the King" Master of Ceremonies in
> 2009 and played for Rev. Cleveland.
> James Cleveland's group was Odessa,
> Roger, and Billy on organ.
> James Cleveland taught Aretha Frank-
> lin how to play the piano and also put
> her father, Rev. C.L. Franklin's radio choir
> together. James Cleveland worked with
> Rev. Charles Ashley Craig, Sr. and the
> One Hundred Voices of Tabernacle. Leslie
> Bush and Alfred Bolden were musicians
> at Prayer Tabernacle Church, where Rev.
> Cleveland recorded "The Love of God."
> He could get any musician.If he got an-
> gry with them, he would get them up
> play himself. James was intelligent. He
> was the "pied piper" of gospel, drawing
> musicians and singers to him. He was
> able to draw people from everywhere.

Mr. Ford reflected on the growth of GMWA
over the years. The Workshop allowed people to travel to different parts of the country
and share gospel music. It was the first time
many from the East Coast had ever been on
the West Coast. He recalls chartering a plane
to fly them there. The year 1972 was a financial turning point for the young organization

because for the first time, GMWA came out of the red into the black.

"The first convention held in New York City (1975) really brought them out of the woods," Ford recalled. It was also during this convention that Rev. Cleveland had a heart attack in Madison Square Garden. He later told the board "I could have died from that heart attack. I'll tell you all right now. I could have died. No moving up when I die. I want the constituents to choose who is capable of taking it [GMWA] up to the next level."

Mr. Ford recalled the period of time following the death of Rev. Cleveland in 1991. Board members were jockeying for leadership positions. He stopped them and reminded them of Rev. Cleveland's wishes regarding his successor, specifically, that parliamentary procedure (1970) wouldn't be followed in replacing him. Instead, GMWA members would elect the board members every two years. The board members would elect a chairman every four years.

One historic GMWA Workshop convention that will never be forgotten was held in Salt Lake City (1991). It was the first time the Mormon Tabernacle had a Hammond organ and drums in its sanctuary. It was also the first time that gospel music and a great number of black people were invited inside the tabernacle. Ford remembers it as being one of the best conventions ever, although only about 5,000 people attended:

> Salt Lake City didn't have the hotel space for a large number of people,

so the number of attendees worked out. GMWA members were dressed in white; The Mormon Tabernacle choir was dressed in light blue. Rev. Charles Adams presided over the consecration.

Mother Reatha Glover, head of the evangelistic board, sang "Lift Him Up" and electrified the audience, surprising many whites who didn't know the history of hymnology in the black church. GMWA delegates knew all the words of the songs the Mormons selected and sung them without sheet music. The Mormons were amazed by the GMWA–both at how the delegates looked in white and the songs they knew.

All who came to Salt Lake City had a great time. Board members were fed free daily and even invited to the governor's mansion. Some Salt Lake City residents visited the hotels where the GMWA members stayed. One resident said that she had never seen so many black people in years and offered to feed the GMWA's 20 board members. True to her word, she returned the next day with a van and a station wagon and took the board members to her home to eat. The board members were told that the whites had been given a class on how to treat the blacks at the convention before they arrived.

Mr. Ford recalls the last tribute that Rev. Cleveland was able to attend. It was the Fiftieth Anniversary Salute to James Cleveland held at Dorothy Chandler Pavilion in 1990. Rev. Cleveland had a tracheotomy at the time. Though weak, he was able to speak and sing a song. Friends and persons whom he had mentored along the way, and who had become gospel stars, accompanied him to his home after the salute. Rev. Cleveland died shortly thereafter.

Mr. Ford received a call from board member Ed Smith on the day that Rev. Cleveland died. Mr. Ford was on the way to sing with the Philadelphia Mass Choir in New Jersey and remembers crying both going and coming from the engagement. He also remembers his pastor's tribute to Rev. Cleveland during that following Sunday at church. Because of his long friendship and association with Rev. Cleveland, Mr. Ford was interviewed by the media after Rev. Cleveland's death.

GMWA and Cornerstone Baptist Church jointly planned Rev. Cleveland's funeral. His burial attire was changed three times. He was dressed in a white suite at the funeral home for public viewing. That was changed to a black tuxedo and cummerbund for the homegoing musical at Cornerstone. He was changed into a beautiful white robe for the public funeral at The Shrine Auditorium.

Jean Irving, mother of La Shone Cleveland, James Cleveland's daughter, picked Mr. Ford up after his arrival in Los Angeles prior to the funeral. They went to the home of James Cleveland to assist in planning the funeral arrangements. To this day, Mr. Ford still remembers his (James Cleveland's) address and phone numbers. He and others went to the funeral home to see that Rev. Cleveland's body was properly prepared. Recalls Mr. Ford:

> Norma Jean Pender, who served as publicity chairperson for GMWA, also worked for a mortuary in Detroit. Norma Jean placed Rev. Cleveland's hands on the Bible as he lay in his coffin. Cornerstone held a homegoing musical to celebrate his life. Television screens were mounted in the parking lot to accommodate the crowd.

According to Ford, members of Cornerstone Church were upset because they felt that the Workshop came to take over the funeral preparations and events.

Questions and speculation abounded after James Cleveland's death about the future of GMWA. Many feared that that the deaths of both James Cleveland and Ed Smith would mean an end to the Workshop. James Ford and Elder Charles Davis suggested the establishment of a finance committee at the board meeting in Charlotte, NC (1991) to manage the finances of GMWA and to ensure that it would go on.

Approximately eight members, including Al Hobbs and Rev. Albert Jamison, took the responsibility for managing GMWA's finances after the death of Ed Smith. Ed Smith previously was in complete control of financial matters. Accountability, after all, had to be established for the expenditure of funds from the Workshop's treasury. Measures were put in place to more efficiently and effectively monitor how funds were spent within the organization, and restrictions were imposed on how individuals received funds for work performed for GMWA.

Dr.Yolanda Freeman
(Personal Interview, September, 2009)

Dr. Yolanda Freeman has been a member of the GMWA from its inception.   Her former husband, Harold Freeman, was a member of the National Board of Directors from 1974 to 1980. She is an active member of GMWA, serving as co-chairperson of the Youth Division and as a youth advisor. She hosts a radio program in Chicago and is a member of GAG. Dr. Freeman is also active in gospel music ministry in the Chicagoland area.

Dr. Freeman knew James Cleveland personally. "Rev. Cleveland had been part of the Thomas A. Dorsey convention," she stated in an interview with the author in September 2009.

> He absorbed everything Professor Dorsey taught him over the years. Rev. Cleveland tried to make Chicago the initial base for GMWA since Chicago has been called the "home of gospel music." Established ministers and groups under the leadership of Rev. Miton Brunson of The Thompson Community Singers helped to prevent this from happening. Milton Brunson instead formed the United Fellowship of Choirs with Father Charles Hayes, Maceo Woods, Lucious Hall, Harold Freeman, and Professor Robert Wooten.

Rev. Freeman confirmed that discernment is a spiritual gift that is always mentioned in describing Rev. Cleveland. The people he chose to form the governing body of GMWA were gifted in administration. Divisions were formed as the need arose. She adds:

> In the beginning, the few members handled many responsibilities. Rev. Cleveland made wise decisions in this area. Harold Smith and The Majestics was a well-known singing group. He was the president of GMWA in the beginning while James Cleveland was the founder. James Cleveland later became both founder and president. Harold Smith had a short term as president. William Sims and Charles Nicks were an integral part of the early organization.

Dr. Freeman provided the history of the GMWA from its inception through the 1970s. "Rev. Isaac Whitmon, a Chicago pastor and National Board Member has been a part of GMWA since the beginning," she related. "The late Rev. Charles Ashley Craig, Sr., Pastor of Prayer Tabernacle in Detroit was also a part of GMWA from its beginning."

She also spoke of others who were there from the beginning: "James Ford, a current board member, played an important role in GMWA. Philly was a major chapter. Murdene Fielding, married to Quincy Fielding Sr., was appointed to the board. Annette May Thomas was the personal secretary of Rev. James Cleveland. Helen Stephens from Northern California was also a board member."

Dr. Freeman remembers especially, the Lighthouse Voices, a white group of the singers that Helen Stephens brought to GMWA: "The choir consisted of four or five groups. This group had wonderful singers. There were four major groups within Northern California who also brought Daryl Coley to GMWA," she continued. "Many singers came from that region and were under the mentorship of Helen Stephens and Steven Roberts. At the time, Rev. Kenneth Ulmer was the second vice president, William Charles Sims was the first vice-president, and Rev. James Cleveland was the Founder."

She reminisces further about the early days of the GMWA:

> In the early days, the schedule of events consisted of morning classes. Mass choir rehearsal took place in the afternoon. The delegates would eat and relax before preparing for the night. Additional academic class sessions were added as the Workshop grew. Advanced levels of previous classes were offered for those who had mastered the basic classes in earlier years. Dr. Sims was instrumental in forming the Academic Division. Just a few classes were offered in the beginning. He developed the very basic courses that would interest the people and effect training in voice, piano, and organ. These classes were at a rudimentary level – totally new –to find out where the interests of people lay. Academics

were a way to give spouses and family members something to do during the day since most of the action took place at night. Workshop participants went back and told others at home about the classes and brought others from their cities. The GMWA Academic Division expanded to include beginner, intermediate, and advanced classes.

Dr. Freeman shared information about people and events during the years when Rev. Cleveland headed the GMWA. "Rev. Reatha Glover, a powerful prophetess from Detroit, was the initial head of the Evangelistic Board. Alma Hendricks Parham was the first person in charge of the women's division, and then Mary K. Elsaw. Theodore King was the first to head the men's division and the Thurston Frazier Chorale. The father of Taft Harris (Houston) - became the first person in charge of security – then one of the Craig brothers."

A group of radio announcers existed under the leadership of Al Hobbs. Rev. Mother (Norma Jean) Pender handled the public relations for GMWA. "She was a powerful announcer out of Detroit who was involved in radio ministry and GMWA from its inception, "Dr. Freeman said. Edna Tatum, a Los Angeles announcer, served as the spokesperson for the announcers until Al Hobbs formalized the guild."

Sara Powell was chair of the Youth Division, and Rev. Freeman became co-chairperson in 1982. Dr. Freeman remembers how Quincy Fielding Jr. pulled together a group of young people and asked Rev. Cleveland to give them permission to participate in the Workshop.

The youth sang one night at the convention and did well. This marked the formation of the youth choir—later to become a component of the Youth Division.

Dean Simmons gave permission to Robert Fryson and Yolanda Freeman to develop youth classes. These classes followed the same structure as the adult convention and were set up to train and develop youth to flow into the adult convention seamlessly. The youth division had nurses, security, a songwriter's component, music kit, tee shirts, and academic classes. The structure required participating youth to take two classes in order to sing in the youth mass choir. The Dr. Robert J. Fryson Memorial Chorale was created as a memorial in his honor after his death. It serves as a feeder for young people in high school and college who chose not to participate in a mass choir but still wanted to sing in a group.

"The objective of the Youth Division was to encourage the young people to continue their learning experiences, realize their potential, prepare them for college, and prepare them to move on. This is not pushed as much as it was in the past." She is concerned that today's youth don't embrace the philosophy that undergirded that division:

> They need to accept the value of education; the vision must be supported. People who don't know the mission and vision have no appreciation for the value of the Workshop. There was a time when children and parents both learned from the experience.

On the bright side, GMWA allows for children who grew up in the organization to assume leadership roles as they become adults. As a case in point, says Dr. Freeman, "Mark Smith, the son of Ed and Sheila Smith, is in charge of operations. Craig Hayes is the current president of the Youth/Young Adult Division. Kim Hardy, a member of the youth liturgical dance program (developed by Berniece Jamison-Turner), now serves as an instructor in the Academic Division. There now exist beginning, intermediate, and advanced praise dance classes that are taught by young people who came up through the Youth/Young Adult Division."

In closing, Dr. Freeman addressed the heritage and legacy of GMWA recalling those who had been a part of the Thomas Dorsey National Convention of Gospel Choirs and Choruses and who later became part of the GMWA: "Donald Lawrence came through Thomas Dorsey; Leonard Burke came through Thomas Dorsey, Quincy Fielding Sr. came through Thomas Dorsey and the GMWA. She also thought of the contemporary gospel artists who are part of GMWA's heritage and who by association, are part of Rev. James Cleveland's legacy: Kurt Carr, Kirk Franklin, Yolanda Adams, John P. Kee, Craig Hayes, Carol Alton, and Myrna Summer.

Elder William Fuqua (Personal Interviews, August 2008 and March, 2011)

Elder William Fuqua is the official GMWA historian. He donated his gospel music archives to the GMWA library. The traveling GMWA library makes research materials available to the membership. He says that the donation was prompted by the Holy Spirit. "This is a power gift – it does not come out of you. Gospel music is for changing communities and as a political communication, and for giving you strength during periods of difficulty."

He has been active in music ministry for many years and has drawn contrasts between the structure of Dorsey's National Convention of Gospel Choirs and Choruses that made it impossible for James Cleveland to exist within it and that of the GMWA, which he later founded.

For one, Professor Dorsey basically wanted to perpetuate the old-fashioned way of singing, and he expected members to show the gift of hospitality by hosting out-of-town delegates to the convention in their homes. This shared hospitality was more feasible with the size of the Thomas Dorsey convention than it would be for GMWA. Learned musicians from universities and colleges established a curriculum at GMWA that was not there before.

Elder Fuqua has collected classical gospel music over many years, affirming that, "in the Bible, music is mentioned from Genesis to Revelation. The Holy Ghost is as much a part of music as the spoken word." His collection includes CDs of gospel groups. It credits the writers of songs so that people give credit where credit is due. The collection of gospel greats include: Thomas Dorsey, James Cleveland, Lucie Campbell, Clara Ward, Roberta Martin, and Alex Bradford.

Elder Fuqua adds materials to the archived collection each year. The library is re-assembled for board meetings and annual conventions. Songs are copyrighted. Writers and arrangers are noted. The important people in gospel music publishing are named and their pictures are displayed with a history of their contribution to gospel music. "It's important to see what people looked like," Elder Fuqua says. "Gospel is the good news, the musical aspects of the Gospel. Music is just as important as the spoken word," he emphasized in his zeal to ensure that the heritage and legacy of GMWA is transmitted to future generations.

"Many people have not been taught to know that there is a divine purpose in music –that it's not for show. That is the main goal of this institution. We must consider the guidance of the Holy Spirit in order for all of us to have the same mind – oneness."

Dr. Joan Hillsman
(Personal Interview, August 2009)

Dr. Joan Hillsman has been a member of GMWA since its inception. In her words, she "stumbled onto the Workshop" when Rev. James Cleveland came to Washington, D.C. She had a musical studio in the same building where the late Rev. Theodore King organized the GMWA's D.C. Chapter. Dr. Hillsman joined the academic faculty during the time when people were recruited "from the floor" at conventions to teach. She first worked with Dr. Charles Sims and then with Dr. R. M. Simmons.

A member of the Board of Directors, Dr. Hillsman currently works in the Academic Division

with Dean Charles F. Reese. She recently implemented and coordinated a "College Night" at
the GMWA Board Meeting in 2010 where students from several colleges attended. It was a
spirit-filled evening. This author was present to
witness the outpouring of God's anointing on
those who participated in the event. There are
plans for College Night to be a permanent part
of GMWA, with the college students invited to
perform at the annual board meetings.

In describing the mission of the GMWA, Dr.
Hillsman says:

> Rev. James Cleveland's focus for the
> Workshop was to create a platform for
> musicians to come together, to fellow-
> ship, to study, to learn and take that
> knowledge back to their churches. It
> was also a platform where fledgling
> artists could showcase their talents.
> Rev. Cleveland encouraged and sup-
> ported the nightly musicals for new
> talent. The delegates would stay at
> the nightly musicals sometimes until
> 2:00 A.M. , encouraging them –regard-
> less of their level of performance. Rev.
> Cleveland envisioned that one day
> Gospeland would be a reality. Perfor-
> mance and academics are very impor-
> tant divisions within GMWA.

Describing the benefits of the GMWA further, she
explains:

> There exists [within the GMWA] a strong
> platform for record industries and re-
> cording artists. One can purchase the ma-

terials and also do extensive networking. The Workshop is more than gospel music, per se. There is an evangelistic board, women and men's council, youth division, quartet division, performance division, academic courses galore, and much more. Some of the most brilliant teachers [in the field] give of their time, service, and talent. Students can also receive college credit through a consortium. There is a traveling library for research, history, and gospel artifacts. The Workshop is like a "filling station for gospel musicians," a place where one can get much of everything they need musically in one place.

Dr. Hillsman strongly agrees with many that gospel music is a ministry.

Look at *Webster's Dictionary*. [Gospel music] is a powerful ministry and vehicle for people. The message in the music – inspires people – is sacred – reaches all walks, creeds, nationalities. Your witness and message affect people. Ministry means service – one functions where one serves. Gospel music is basic. Although there are different styles, gospel music is now in the mainstream.

Speaking of a performance that she attended in recent years in which a secular Rap artist testified that he had given his life to Christ, she says: "That was due to the power of the ministry of gospel. The artist said that he had come off the streets to minister through gospel rap. The gospel music industry has provided a smorgasbord of music – just like going shopping – gospel reaches all nationalities," she adds.

She emphasized the ministry of gospel music manifested by and made possible through GMWA:

> Gospel music has reached across boundaries and has an international appeal shown by the number of people across the world who come to the Workshop. There are several international chapters within GMWA. Some have even converted to Christianity from this experience. Gospel music permeates all boundaries. The gospel is very powerful.

Her outlook for the future of GMWA is that the Workshop will continue disseminating music, research, history, and gospel performance techniques throughout the world. The components to achieve this are already present within the Workshop. She foresees gospel music becoming even more recognized as a valid art form.

Rev. Brenda Hollins
(Personal Interview, February, 2010)

Rev. Brenda Hollins serves as co-pastor of The Revealing M.B. Church in Chicago where her husband Rev. James Hollins, Sr. is pastor. Rev. Hollins is on the national Evangelistic Board of the GMWA and is an active community leader in Chicago and Executive

Director of the R.B.C. Community Service Center. Commercials featuring the work of her organization are currently aired on the website of the Museum of Science and Industry in Chicago as well as on the major networks, including OWN.

Rev. Hollins became a part of the Workshop in 1981 and joined the Evangelistic Board in 1984. She has attended most of the board meetings over the years. The late Chicago Chapter Representative, Essie Johnson Lane, appointed her to become chairperson of the Chicago Metro Evangelistic Ministry Chapter in the 1990s. Mother Glover, the bastion of the evangelical board at the national level for many years, mentored and pushed Rev. Hollins. She became a licensed and ordained minister by 1994.

"I had always heard Rev. Cleveland's music and bought his albums," Rev. Hollins confided. "I wanted him to sing at my funeral. His music was my connection with church in my younger years," she explained, saying that his musicals brought her comfort.

She remembers Rev. Cleveland as "a real person who knew no strangers," recalling that he would tell nervous singers when asked to perform on the national stage to 'sing your hit.' "Rev. Cleveland spoke and brought things into perspective," she mused.

Rev. Hollins shared these words about her mentor, Rev. Reatha Glover:

Mother Glover was an extremely gifted woman of God. She resigned from her position with national

GMWA around 2005. Mother Reatha Glover was from Detroit, and a member of Rev. Nicks' church. She was appointed by Rev. Cleveland to take leadership of evangelism at the national convention. She was a prophet, an administrator, a teacher and a missionary. Mother Glover was bold in her prophecy; she walked in her calling and stood on whatever the Lord gave her. She didn't back down when giving counsel. She demonstrated the gifts of teaching, nurturing, wisdom, and discernment. Mother Glover's desire was for the ministry to be profitable to the members personally as well as to the community it served. The power of her anointing was so strong that people would come to her for anointing and blessings on Friday, the last day of the Workshop. She would lay hands on persons and prophesize as God gave utterance. She saw beneath the veil as she ministered to others. Three people were chosen to continue the work that she had always done upon her retirement.

The Evangelistic Board is overseen now by Elder Eugene Bryant from Los Angeles. Rev. Anita O'Brien, and Elder Berniece Jamison-Turner serve as his assistants.

"These three," says Rev. Hollins, "came up under Mother Glover's teaching. They have brought more structure to the duties of the evangelistic board during the convention week. Among its duties are administering the sacraments at the opening Sunday consecration service. The board members also serve as intercessors for delegates during the convention week. Auxiliary meetings are scheduled throughout the week from Monday through Thursday. Planned activities benefit the members personally and for their ministry at home."

Rev. Hollins recognizes the contribution of one of the past leaders of the Evangelistic Board: "The late Barbara Brown of California was responsible for establishing an outreach mission project in every city that the Workshop met in throughout the history of the convention," she revealed.

"This began in the Cleveland years and has continued with Bishop Jamison. The evangelistic committee contacts the local chairperson of the convention city, who helps to identify a place in the community to feed the homeless. Flyers are distributed the Monday before, giving the place and time for the meal distributions. The meals are served on Tuesdays and Wednesday of convention week. A word from Scripture consecrates the meal."

Rev. Hollins added that a budget was finally established by the national governing board for this annual outreach project.

Rev. Hollins, in reflection, speaks of the changes brought about by the growth of the Workshop over the years. She concedes that the changes have been good and bad. She understands that GMWA's growth has changed the small intimate setting that marked the early conventions.

The Friday night concert was the
high point of the Workshop for me.
Rev. James Cleveland would lead
"Till We Meet Again." Rev. Richard
"Mr. Clean" White led the song after
Rev. Cleveland's death. It was a very
powerful experience for the delegates
as they left to return to their home
states. The generation who relied on
that song is dying out. The younger
generation doesn't seem to know the
song nor understand the meaning and
significance it held in the past. That is
something that can never be re-invent-
ed – it's gone. Many delegates left with
tears in their eyes. That song had great
emotional impact for us. That service
was so filled with God's spirit. That
fellowship has changed – that kindred
spirit is different. Growth brings with
it a new spirit and attitude. Attempts
to bring that song back have failed
over the years – but now – people
don't know the song. The Convention
isn't the same fellowship. Individual
divisions have their close fellowship
but it isn't felt within the full convention. In reality however, the convention is a very powerful forum for artists, performers, and leaders. There is
something for everyone.

She still wishes there was enough time
within the week's activities to attend musicals
of the different divisions. She has yet to attend a quartet division musical.

Rev. Hollins concluded the interview with these words:

> Rev. Cleveland's vision is his legacy. He envisioned meeting the needs of gospel music and church ministry in its entirety– years before it became a reality.

Bishop Jamison's legacy is meeting the needs of the new millennium – the demands of the 21st century, seeing the challenges in the industry yet maintaining the chapter's integrity. He saw that the corporate musicians were stifling the spiritual atmosphere and fellowship of the chapters. He brought it back to the chapters – making it once again "our convention." The convention is designed to meet the needs of every delegate in all dimensions.

Mr. Eugene Morgan
(Personal Interview, July, 2009)

Eugene Morgan has been a part of GMWA for 30 years and a member of the Academic Division for 18 of those years. A retired educator, Mr. Morgan is responsible for the academic robing of faculty members and for faculty protocol. He also serves as a class supervisor in the Academic Division and facilitates the F-826 Fundamentals class on the history and development of the GMWA, a class that is beneficial for all Workshop participants. Mr. Morgan envisions it ideally as a course that is taught in segments each year until the entire history is complete. This course should be a pre-requisite, he believes.

Mr. Morgan has watched the convention grow from an attendance of about 18,000 to 28,000.

"GMWA continues to go boldly into the future," he stated in an interview. He hopes that the convention's change to July will attract more young people, as elders of the convention are dying each year. He enjoys traveling to the different cities where "people are empowered to do what they've never done before. One's experience is broadened by visiting different places – diversity, different ways of expressing things – but with a common goal," he says.

The Gifts of the Spirit that Mr. Morgan identifies as manifest in GMWA are evangelism, a divinely inspired faculty, giving, faith, shepherding, compassion, and providing aid through outreach activities.

Said Mr. Morgan, "GMWA embraced President Obama's challenge to volunteer in the community. Ron Mangus, GMWA legal counsel, led the outreach in Cincinnati in 2011, and it will continue in future years. The first outreach saw approximately 200 GMWA members from the nation volunteering in the communities of Cincinnati. The gifts of aid and helps were evident as people were fed, patients in hospitals were visited, and the message of the gospel was preached in the process. The Spirit of evangelism was present in that outreach," he added.

A helper and an intercessor, Mr. Morgan prays for the GMWA daily. His desire is for GMWA to be used as a conduit to encourage the Body of Christ as expressed in the words of Philippians 4:13. The scripture "I can do all things through Christ, who strengthens me," is a Scripture that leads me daily," reflects Mr. Morgan.

Evangelist Dr. Eva J. Purnell
(Personal Interviews, June, 2009, February, 2011)

Dr. Eva J. Purnell, an early gospel legend, was honored at the 2007 Chicago Gospel Fest as a "living gospel legend." She is Minister-of-Music Emeritus at Memorial M.B. Church in Chicago. She was a member of the pioneering Inspirational Singers with Almond Dawson. The group was one of the early pioneer gospel groups presented on Sid Ordower's "Jubilee Showcase." Dr. Purnell quips that she was "saved by a song – not a sermon." She shared these observations concerning the gospel music ministry:

> The spiritual gifts of gospel music are discernment and exhortation. James Cleveland possessed those spiritual gifts and was much anointed as evidenced by his music. Discernment in gospel music is a gift that operates in the soul of the minister of music or director. He or she has the gift to discern the music that is needed to speak to the congregation's heart and needs in a way a hymn cannot. The hymns are generally chosen for morning worship and may or may not meet the felt needs of the people.

Dr. Purnell elaborates on the types of sacred music by defining corporate music in the following terms:

> Vertical music sings to God. Examples include hymns and anthems. Gospel music is lateral; it sings to people about

their experiences. The song "The Lord Will Make a Way Somehow" tells believers that the Lord will bring them out. Gospel music in its flexibility allows you to have more selections that go from people to people, heart to heart, and breast to breast.

Dr. Purnell was part of the first gospel music programming done in the United States. Chicago was the birthplace of televised gospel programs, where Jubilee Showcase, the first show dedicated to the genre aired. The Inspirational Singers were a part of that history. "No non church program did that" states Dr. Purnell. "They just highlighted gospel singers."

When she was asked if spiritual gifts are still manifested in gospel recording artists, Evangelist Purnell replied that [today's] gospel music artists are commercial. When asked if the gospel is preached only or both preached and sung, she said, "When Paul and Silas were in jail, the early church was singing and praying. [Thus] the gospel is both sung and preached."

Dean Charles F. Reese
(Personal Interview, July, 2009)

Dr. Charles F. Reese is the Dean of the Academic Division of the Gospel Music Workshop of America, Inc. and also a member of the organization's National Board of Directors. He has been affiliated with GMWA for 35 years. He is the author of The *Historical Foundation, Formation and Development—From a Dream and a Vision- 2nd Revision* by Dr. Charles F. Reese (2008, 2009) that details the origin and history of GMWA, Inc. His primary responsibility as dean is to upgrade the offerings of the Academic Department and to make it competitive in the field of music education.

Dean Reese says that from a holistic viewpoint – cohesiveness holds the GMWA together. "This cohesiveness operates throughout the entire organization," he added. Dr. Reese said that administration, serving, teaching, exhortation, helps, and giving aid and discernment were the gifts given to him [to be used] for the body of GMWA. These are gifts delineated in 1 Corinthians 12, Ephesians 6, and Romans 12 for the members of the Body of Christ.

Dean Reese shares his vision for the future of GMWA. Education is of paramount importance in achieving this result. Dean Reese's ultimate goal is for GMWA to become an accredited degree-granting institution, a reality that he sees achievable within the next five years. The preliminary and core-inspections to this end have been completed. The current plan has developed more than the original scope (Gospeland). General music, ethnomusicology and theomusicology will be included in the course offerings.

Ethnomusicology pertains to the effect of one's cultural heritage on one's music. It compares the influence of music among different cultures. Theomusicology, however, pertains to the effect of one's culture, sacred traditions, religious customs, symbols and myths on one's worship experience and belief.

Dean Reese spoke of the growth that has taken place over the years within the academic department. He has watched it grow from a volunteer cadre of instructors to a department with credentialed, experienced teachers. Its professionalization is manifested by the outstanding qualifications of the faculty. He addressed the dedication of teachers who do not receive compensation commensurate with the quality of teaching that they offer during the Workshop and surmised that this dedication isn't true of other conventions.

Dr. Reese offered this observation in speaking of the men who worked tirelessly in the early years to ensure the success and continuation of GMWA:

> These persons added tremendously to the success of the organization: Rev. James Cleveland (Founder and President); Professor Charles Sims, (1st Vice President); Mr. Edward Smith (Executive Secretary); Rev. Charles Nicks(2nd Vice –President); Dr. Robert M. Simmons (Dean 1975-1999); Elder Charles Davis (former Board Secretary, national board member); and Mr. James Ford (past Board of Directors liaison for the National Mass Choir and national board member). All have passed but the last two named.

Rev. Sam Roberson
(Personal Interview, March, 2010)

Rev. Sam Roberson is Pastor of Community Baptist Church in Henderson, Nevada. He was a radio broadcaster for 30 years until 1997 and still serves on the advisory board of

KCEP. Rev. Roberson is also very active in the state and National Baptist Convention.

Rev. Roberson opened GMWA's first chapter in Las Vegas in 1975. He operated a music bookstore and was approached by Ed Smith, who was in Las Vegas for a GMWA board meeting. Smith had asked locals in Las Vegas for the name of someone who might help him bring a GMWA chapter to the city, and Sam Roberson was recommended. GMWA had between 8,000 and 10,000 members at the time.

"The GMWA board meeting was held at the Doolittle Recreational Center's gymnasium. There were problems with sound quality at the gymnasium that affected the performance of singers and choirs," recalled Rev. Roberson. "Rev. Cleveland sung 'Jesus Is the Best Thing [That Ever Happened to Me],' but he didn't record it there."

Rev. Roberson served as co-chapter representative of the Silver State Chapter with Charles Holder. He was also a member of the Gospel Announcers Guild (GAG). His active participation in GMWA ended in 1986.

Rev. Roberson reminisces about his time in GAG: "I worked with Al Hobbs on the Arizona, Nevada, and Southern California (Region Six) of GAG. Members of GAG networked and shared information with each other," he says, recalling the GAG's motto: 'Appreciating our own—respecting our own music.'"

Recalling Rev. James Cleveland, Rev. Roberson said: "Rev. Cleveland demanded respect from the members of GMWA. By his insistence that "what [happens] backstage stays backstage," he demanded that artists respect each other. "Delegates had to remain seated or wait outside while groups were performing."

Rev. Cleveland was deeply respected by the GMWA membership. In Rev. Roberson's opinion, James Cleveland, Charles Nicks Jr., and Mattie Moss, deserve credit for putting GMWA together. He also cited the contribution of gospel singers and churches who supported GMWA.

Rev. Roberson prizes GMWA as a national gospel music organization, praising it in these words: "GMWA is the mother of all organizations. It sets the standard in offering and giving new artists a platform and providing a built-in audience for them ."

He remembered Vanessa Bell Armstrong's appearance at GMWA before she became a recording artist and recalled performers who had been part of gospel before it became popular, before it was broadcast or televised, emphasizing that "during the lean years, there was someone before Kirk Franklin: Ira Tucker and the Dixie Hummingbirds. Helen Stephens wiped out the audience in North Carolina with the white group – singers who sounded like us. Cassietta George of the Caravans joined in with them."

He spoke of Rev. Cleveland's vision for Gospeland: One hundred acres of donated land that would house meeting facilities and include a library with history and video collections of gospel music's performers, including Dorsey's Collection, and a university. He [Cleveland] wanted a place where we could "showcase" our own. Rev. Robeson recalled that one of Cleveland's spiritual gifts was his ability to involve his friends in the GMWA music ministry.

On the topic of changes in gospel music from traditional to contemporary, Roberson considered the distinctions between "old school," "new school," and "hip-hop."

"Sometime I crave the old music," he mused. "New music has its purpose: once you bring them to church, you must have a message. If this helps them think, then it serves its purpose."

Rev. Roberson would like to see a city-wide revival for the youth. This effort would enable them to come in off the streets. He ended in saying that "a concerted effort is needed to reach those on the streets with the message of salvation."

Dr. Steven Roberts
(Personal Interview, August, 2009)

Dr. Roberts resides in Northern California. He is a musician and musical leader in California and conducts workshops around the country. He has been a part of GMWA since its inception, and was among the persons chosen for the Leadership Identification Program instituted by Rev. Cleveland. The purpose of the program was to identify and train participants in the convention who had promising gifts and attributes for ministry and service to the Workshop. These candidates were enrolled in a rigorous five-year program. At least two hours each day were spent shadowing a board member.

Dr. Jones saw the spirit of well-being spread in the Workshop through these shadowings. He also observed the different spiritual gifts manifested by the board members. All had a deep respect for God, the church, and God's agenda.

Roberts graduated from the program in 1987, and he put his Workshop training to use by becoming Dr. Rodena Preston's assistant in directing the Mass Choir. Ultimately, he assumed leadership for its day-to-day operations.

Both he and Dr. Margaret Douroux were presented the Alma Hendricks Award at the GMWA National Workshop in 1992 for the 13 or 14 songs they wrote that were recorded by the National Mass Choir. A great honor, Dr. Roberts remembers when he dreamed of being a part of this team (GMWA): "Little did I know this would make a difference," he says.

He was appointed to the National Board of Directors of GMWA in 2009. In addition, he has the responsibility for leading the James Cleveland Choir. Reflecting on the spiritual gifts of James Cleveland, he says:

> The legacy of Cleveland was in helping other people – not for self-glorification, but for others. His untimely death changed the legacy. Every night in the Workshop, he spoke of God's awesomeness. He would come up, work the crowd with a song, and sit at the piano. Concert virtuosos would play up and down the piano scales, but the building went into a hush when Cleveland sat at the piano. He could play with one finger, and the atmosphere changed when he played. The sincerity and deepness of his love-relationship with God showed in his work.

He was unpretentious. He would stand, adjust his glasses, and take his time. He might begin with: "I don't know...." (Now he has the audience's attention.) "But sometimes I get—I have moments where I just wonder where God is..." He would then bring in a real circumstance, come up with a song that turns everything all around.

Dr. Roberts commented on the careers that Rev. Cleveland empowered:

He played a very active role in advancing the careers of several people. He would ask unknown musicians to play or sing. That mere act would revive that musician's career. I've seen it done for many people. He'd put his arm around them – ask them to sing a line, and it turned their musical career around.

The 1989 board meeting in Mobile, Alabama, marked the last time those who built up GMWA would be together (all would be dead within the next ten years). Roberts described how Rev. Cleveland used the night services to minister to the audience:

He could discern the spiritual needs of those present and would prophesy to different people. Charles Nicks Jr., friend of Rev. Cleveland, accomplished organist, composer, preacher, and GMWA pioneer, would play something, and Rev. Cleveland would go wherever the Spirit took

Rev. Nicks. Rev. Cleveland could walk up to the person and minister to his or her need and start admonishing, lifting the person with a testimony that showed the power of God's healing. Where else can you go to be in an atmosphere like this? Little did we know that would be the last time that the board all would be together—all would be gone within ten years: Charles Nicks, Rev. Cleveland, Ed Smith, Donald Vails, Robert Fryson, Mary Kay Elsaw, and Quincy Fielding, Sr.

Steven Roberts is concerned that successors aren't prepared to follow in the leaders' footsteps, a flaw seen over and over in churches that leads to disharmony when the leader dies. Dr. Roberts stated that Rev. Cleveland was known for the gifts of discernment and wisdom. "He always associated with people in the know. The Academic Division wouldn't be what it is without Dr. Simmons – who put Dean Reese in place – and was an icon in the Workshop. Dr. Simmons was a visionary who looked into the future and entirely revamped the Academic Division. "You must have enough wisdom to know and understand how to live. Knowledge, fear of God and reverence for Him and others was seen in the three founding fathers, Ed Smith, Charles Nicks, and Rev. James Cleveland."

Roberts comments on the changes in the Workshop over the years:

The emphasis of music ministry has shifted over the years. Musicians want to be paid for their talent. Church musicians sometimes refer to their church position as 'a gig.' A songwriterwho presents at the Workshop receives only about 50 percent of the proceeds from the song. That may be discouraging for some new songwriters. Ministers and musicians are sometimes at odds.

He recalled an article in the *Atlanta Journal-Constitution* three to four years ago in which the musician referred to a change in venue as being the nature of the business. "It's about advancement – not about God. If I were a pastor, there would be basic ground rules. Too many musicians and pastors are at war. It destroys the church when the musician leaves."
Dr. Roberts adds, "It is very important to watch and observe the mindset of the musician – [whether there is] reverence for God or God's people."
Roberts has played for three churches. He makes love the bottom line: "You must possess 'God love.' The first people you show it to are other Christians. The love that you show one another – that's how the world knows that you are a disciple. There is no other way the Scripture says you will be known."
Dr. Roberts has observed the influence of corporate industry in the Workshop. Ministry sometimes becomes strictly industry. Talents are often seen, but not spiritual gifts. He makes a clear distinction between spiritual gifts and natural talents.

"Until we recapture that Spirit of God first, others second, and me after that, we will be struggling in some of these areas," he says.

In concluding the interview, Dr. Roberts sees inclusion as the necessary model for the future of GMWA. He envisions auxiliary leaders giving input to decisions made by the chairman and the board for the operational planning and oversight of GMWA. He mentioned other early leaders, including Mary K. Elsaw, who charted the direction of divisions within the organization. He regrets that Rev. Cleveland wasn't taped in the early years:

> That era is lost to future generations because the capacity for digitalization was lacking. No one thought to tape the nightly services, and that past is lost forever. The Workshop must, however, train and build up the membership for the good of the body. Seeds must be planted for the future. Input and consensus from delegates, auxiliary and division leaders, board members, with the chairman Bishop Jamison, are necessary for the continued growth and spirituality of the Workshop.

Mattie Robertson
(Personal Interview, August 2009)

Mrs. Mattie Robertson is a member of the Academic Faculty and also serves as a Thurston Frazier Chorale Director. She is active in music ministry at her late uncle's church, First Baptist Church in Chicago, and the North Shore

Chapter of GMWA. She also served in music ministry at Metropolitan Missionary Baptist Church on Chicago's West Side for 65 years.

Mrs. Robertson comes from a Levitical family. Her mother, one of nine children, and her grandmother loved music. This love was instilled into all the children who either play, sing or do both within music ministry.

In this interview, Mrs. Robertson discussed the different musical genres, and is of the opinion that many people don't understand the different genres of music. She explains:

> Psalms were used by the musicians to usher the Spirit into the temple through music. Gospel music is inspired by people with a deep feeling for God – from within – through experiences they have had. It is more inspirational than it is Biblical.
>
> An anthem is purely the Word of God. The use of the anthem form doesn't make a composition an anthem. The 150th Psalm, for example, has many arrangements of that scripture.

She recalls her mother going to the Sunday School Congress where people were asked to write down their favorite hymn. "Not all of them were hymns – some were their favorite songs," she said. She also makes a distinction concerning our Negro spiritual heritage. "Spirituals are categorized as Negro spirituals–that is what they are."

Mrs. Robertson arranges hymns because they inspire her. She exclaims, "To be inspired by music is a gift. Rev. James Cleveland didn't have a degree in music, but his music was inspired by God."

In expressing her love for Rev. Cleveland and his music, Mrs. Robertson says: "James Cleveland insisted that the convention be Christ like—only worshipping the Christ. He really kept that in front of us."

Speaking of the addition of "Daily Bread" by Bishop Jamison, she says: "Daily Bread is like a retreat because of all the inspirational speakers." She also referred to GMWA's classical division—the Thurston Frazier Chorale, exclaiming that there is something for everyone

She also expressed admiration for the academic faculty. "Delegates are anxious to sit under those wonderful people. The faculty has many PhDs on staff that provide wonderful learning experiences for all musicians."

She beams when referring to a class she teaches. "It is a phenomenal sacred music class that gives me the very diverse music that I want. Composers come in to present music that they write—genres from anthems to gospel. Classes are provided for musicians throughout the workshop."

She recalls a specific highlight from the early years:

> Helen Stephens, from Northern California, directed the Berkeley group–
> a fabulous choir from the university.
> Helen told how she had led white students –Hippies, as they were known
> then—to Christ. She brought them to
> the convention. They sang "Jesus is the

Center of My Joy" and brought down the house. That ecumenical flavor shows that we (African Americans) aren't the only ones that God inspires or touches.

Mattie Robertson's vision is that GMWA continue its influence in the gospel music industry after some soul-searching. She can't wait to go to the convention each year. "Associations are formed within the workshop between people and the networking is amazing," she says. She cites love as the driving force that binds delegates together in the Workshop.

"Love is the ingredient. Love comes from God. GMWA is a place 'Where Everybody Is Somebody.' A diversity of people comes to the Workshop. People are determined—that's what makes it so wonderful –God makes a way for them. Christ can do anything."

Rev. Spencer White
(Personal Interview, March, 2010)

Rev. Spencer White serves as an associate pastor of the International Church of Las Vegas. Its lead pastors are Paul and Denise Goulet. He has been a member of the Las Vegas Chapter for 15 years and has served in a leadership position for the past 10 years as Chapter Representative of the Silver State Chapter. He also serves as Second Vice President of the Executive Board of Chapter Representatives of GMWA.

Rev. White's desire is that GMWA continue the legacy and focus of Rev. James Cleveland. He speaks of the place traditional gospel holds for him personally, describing Rev. Cleveland's music as "the kind of music that gets down in your soul...makes you honor God and give Him thanks and glory...makes you excited – sticks with you—stirs up that inner man".

He calls this type of music as "something we grew up with – that no one can take it away from you. James Cleveland wrote so many songs that aren't even sung," he says. "The James Cleveland Choir sings nothing but his songs."

Rev. White has a great love and passion for gospel music as expressed in his words in this interview. He has been involved in gospel music his entire life and currently uses his spiritual gifts by mentoring the Georgia, Nebraska, Pennsylvania, and Rhode Island Chapters.

The GMWA conventions are uplifting to him. His vision for GMWA concerned the next generation. He discerns a need for youth to become more involved in the organization. His goal is that GMWA "embrace the next generation to carry on gospel music."

Bibliography

Books

Allen, William Francis, Charles Pickard Ware, Lucy McKim Garrison, eds. *Slave Songs of the United States*. New York: A. Simpson & Co., 1867.

The American Heritage® Dictionary of the English Language, Fourth Edition. Boston: Houghton Mifflin Company, 2009.

Banfield, William C. *Cultural Codes Making of a Black Music Philosophy*, Lanham: Scarecrow Press, Inc., 2010.

Barney, Deborah Verdice. *The Gospel Announcer and the Black Gospel Music Tradition*. Ann Arbor: UMI, 1994.

Batastini, Robert J., exec. ed. *African American Heritage Hymnal*. Chicago: GIA Publications, 2001.

Bowen, O.W., G.A Moerner, eds. *Better Music in the Church, Rev. Edition*. New York: Abingdon-Cokesbury Press, 1944.

Boyer, Horace Clarence (text), and Lloyd Yearwood (photography). *How Sweet the Sound: the Golden Age of* Washington, D.C: Elliott & Clark 1995.

Caldwell, Hansonia L. *African American Music a Chronology* 1619-1995. Culver City, CA: IKORO Communication, Inc, 1995.

Carpenter, Bill. *Uncloudy Days: the Gospel Music Encyclopedia*. San Francisco: Backbeat Books, 2005.

The Celebration Hymnal: Songs *and Hymns for Worship.* The National Baptist Publishing Board. Nashville: Triad Publications, 1977.

Collins, Lisa. *The Gospel Music Industry Round-Up.* Los Angeles: Eye on Gospel Publications, 2009.

Columbia Encyclopedia. *The Columbia Electronic Encyclopedia, Sixth Edition.* New York: Columbia University Press, 2011.

Cone, James H. *Liberation: A Black Theology of Liberation.* Philadelphia: Lippincott, 1970.

Cone, James *The Spirituals and the Blues: Interpretations.* Harrisburg: Seabury Press, 1971.

Darden, Robert. *People Get Ready a New History of Black Gospel Music.* New York: Continuum International Publishing Group Inc., 2004.

Doane,W.H., E.H. Johnson, A. J. Rowland, P. S. Henson, L.P. Hornderger, eds. *The Baptist Hymnal.* Philadelphia: American Baptist Publishing Society, 1883.

Drake, St. Clair. *Churches and Voluntary Associations in the Chicago Negro Community.* Chicago: Works Progress Administration, 1940.

DuBois, W.E.B. *The Souls of Black Folk.* New York: Bantam Books, 1989.

Dupree Sherry Sherrod and Herbert C. DuPree. *African American Good News (Gospel) Music.* Washington, D.C: Middle Atlantic Regional Press, 1993.

Easton, MG. *Easton's Bible Dictionary*. Nashville: Thomas Nelson Publishers, 1897.

Flynn, Leslie B. *Nineteen Gifts of the Spirit*. Colorado Springs: Chariot Victor Publishing, 1974.

Franklin, Marion Joseph. *The Relationship of Black Preaching to Black Gospel Music.*, Ann Arbor: UMI, 1992

Gingrich, Roy E. *The Gifts of the Spirit*. Memphis: Riverside Printing, 2003.

Harris, Michael. *The Rise of Gospel Blues: The Music of Thomas Andrew Dorsey in the Urban Church*. New York: Oxford University Press, 1992.

Heilbut, Anthony. *The Gospel Sound: Good News and Bad Times*. New York: Limelight Editions, 1985.

Hillsman, Joan R. *Gospel Music: An African American Art Form*. New York: McGraw Hill, 1998.

Hinson, Glenn. *Fire in My Bones: Transcendence and the Holy Spirit in African American Gospel*. Philadelphia: University of Pennsylvania Press, 2000.

Hirsch, E. D., Jr., Joseph F. Kett, and James Trefil, eds. *Dictionary, of Cultural Literacy: Fine Arts. The New Dictionary of Cultural Literacy, Third Edition*. Boston: Houghton Mifflin Company, 2002.

Jackson, Jerma. *Testifying at the Cross: Thomas Andrew Dorsey, Sister Rosetta Tharpe and the Politics of African American Sacred and Secular Music*. Ann Arbor: UMI, 1995.

Johnston, M, ed. *Songs of Zion Supplemental Worship Resources* 12. Nashville: Abingdon Parthenon Press, 1981.

Lindsay, T.M. *International Standard Bible Encyclopedia.* Edited by James Orr.
Nashville: Thomas Nelson Publishers, 1913

Lindsell, Harold, ed. Harper *Study Bible The Holy Bible Revised Standard Version.* New York: Harper & Row Publishers, 1962.

McNeil, W.K., ed. *Encyclopedia of American Gospel Music.* New York: Routledge, 2005.

Morgan, Robert J. *Then Sings My Soul: 150 of the World's Greatest Hymn Stories.* Nashville: Thomas Nelson Publishers, 2003.

Noble, E. Myron. *The Gospel of Music: A Key to Understanding a Major Choir of Ministry.* Washington, D.C.: Mid-Atlantic Press of the Apostolic Faith Churches of God, Inc, 1986.

Osbeck, Kenneth W. *The Ministry of Music.* Grand Rapids: Kregel Publications, 1998.

Oxford Grove Music Encyclopedia. The Concise Grove Dictionary of Music. New York: Oxford University Press, Inc., 1994.

Peretti, Burton W. *Lift Every Voice: The History of African American Music.* New York: Rowman and Littlefield Publishers, 2009.

Pollard, Deborah Smith. *When the Church Becomes Your Party (Contemporary Gospel Music).* Detroit: Wayne State University Press, 2008.

Reagon, Bernice Johnson. *If You Don't Go, Don't Hinder Me: The African American Sacred Song Tradition* from The Abraham Lincoln Lecture Series. Lincoln: University of Nebraska Press, 2001.

Reese, Charles F. *The Gospel Music Workshop of America, Inc: The Historical Foundation and Development from a Dream and a Vision.* Detroit: Gospel Music Workshop of America, Inc., [2004] 2008-2009.

Roach, Hildred. *Black American Music Past and Present, 2nd ed.* Malabar: Krieger Publishing Company, 1992.

Rodeheaver, Homer. *The Book of American Negro Spirituals, James Weldon Johnson,* ed. New York: Viking Press, 1925.

Rodeheaver, Homer. *Southland Spirituals.* Winona Lake: The Rodeheaver Press, 1936.

Simmons, R.M. *Evangelism in Church Music.* Lexington: Young Printing Co., 1976.

Simmons, R.M. *Good Religion Expressions of Energy in Traditional African-American Worship.* Columbus: Laymen Christian Leadership Publication, 1998.

Simmons, R.M. *Perspectives of Praise and Worship.* Dayton: Laymen Christian Leadership Publication, 1997.

Thomas Dorsey on the Precious Lord Story and Gospel Songs. Bloomington: Indiana University School of Music.

Vine, W.E. *Vines' Expository Dictionary of New Testament Word, "Ministering, Ministration, Ministry"* Blue Letter Bible, 1940, 1 April 2007, 8 May 2009

Walton, A.R., H. F. Morris, and J.M. Hinson. *The Complete Church Hymnal.* Atlanta: J.M. Hinson Music Company, 1923.

Warren, Gwendolyn Sims. *Ev'ry Time I Feel the Spirit.* New York: Henry Holt and Company, 1998.

Articles

Adler, Jerry. *Newsweek.* Feb. 8, 1993: 56.

Ankeny, *Billboard Magazine.* Feb. 1003.

Boyer, Horace Clarence. "Gospel Music Comes of Age." *Black World* 23, 1 (1973) 42-48, 70-86.

Collins, Lisa. 1993. "Gospel Pioneer Thomas A. Dorsey Dies: Father of Gospel Music." *Billboard Magazine.*

Granger, Tom. March 1993: 4. "Gospel Pioneer." *Contemporary Christian Music.*

Hampton, Marcus. *Score Magazine.* Jan/Feb. 1993: 12.

Richardson, Cheryl Jenkins. *Chicago Sun Times*: Monday February 1, 1993, 27 Weekend Review "Gospel: A Tribute Fit for a Legend".

Shapiro, Beatrice Michaels. 1993. "Sunday Voices." *Chicago Tribune Magazine.*

Williams, Adina. "A Czech in the Land of Spirituals." *American Legacy: Special Music Edition.*(Summer 2009).

American Legacy: Special Music Edition. (Summer 2009). "Cross-over Pioneer Rosetta Tharpe.

Chicago Tribune Magazine, 1993. "His Word Was Gospel."

Chicago Sunday Tribune, February 10, 1991. "Obituary of James Cleveland."

Dollars & Sense: 9 (April/May) 1983. "The Black Music Experience."

Ebony Magazine 24, 1 (November 1968): 74

Ebony Magazine 22, 12 (October 1967): 48

Ebony Magazine 23, 2 (October 1968): 29

Ebony Magazine 24, 1 (November 1968): 82

Ebony Magazine 24, 3 (January 1969): 14

Ebony Magazine 27, 7 (May 1972): 161

Ebony Magazine 28, (November 1972):

Ebony Magazine 45, 11 (September 1990): 22

Ebony Magazine 28, 1 (November 1972): 86

Ebony Magazine 37, 11 (September 1982): 57

Ebony Magazine 39, 2 (December 1983): 37

Ebony Magazine 40, 2 (1984): 128, 149

Ebony Magazine 41, 5 (March 1986):

Ebony Magazine 45, 11 (September 1990): 22

Bibliography

Ebony Magazine 47, 7 (May 1992):

Ebony Magazine (July 1995): 30

Ebony Magazine 57, 9 (July 2002)

Jet Magazine 79, 21 (3-11-90): 129-130

Jet Magazine 41, 5 (10-28-71): 42

Jet Magazine (5-29-1975): 62

Jet Magazine (8-06-1981): 64

Jet Magazine 61, 6 (10-22-198): 32

Jet Magazine 79, 19 (2-25-1991): 60

Jet Magazine 79, 21 (3-11-90): 129-130

Jet Magazine 107, 10 (3-07-06): 59

Jet Magazine 110, 5 (2-05-07): 36

Organizations

Gospel Music Association Christian Music Networking Guide. Nashville: GMA Association, 1997.

Gospel Music Workshop of America, Inc. *25th Silver Anniversary. Program Book.* Chicago, August 8-15, 1992.

The Gospel Music Workshop of America, Inc., *43rd Annual National Convention Program Book.* Cincinnati, July 24-30, 2010.

Welcome to The Gospel Music Workshop of America (GMWA) Metropolitan Chicago Chapter (Brochure) Evergreen Park: 2009.

The Seventy-Fifth National Convention of Gospel Choirs and Choruses Souvenir Journal. Chicago, August 2-8, 2008.

National Museum of American History Smithsonian Institution. Bernice Johnson Reagon Director, Program in Black American Culture. *Classic Gospel Song*: "A Tribute to Thomas A. Dorsey." Washington, D.C., 1985.

Papers

Fuqua, William R "A Brief Historical Account of Black Gospel Music." Detroit: 1997.

Kalil, Timothy Michael. "The Role of the Great Migration of African Americans to Chicago in the Development of Traditional Black Gospel Piano by Thomas A. Dorsey." Ann Arbor: UMI Dissertation Services, 1993.

Kemp, Kathryn. "A Knowledge Theory Applied to Objective/Subjective Change through a Counselor Training Program." Ann Arbor: UMI, 1983.

Documentaries and Music

Eyes on the Prize: American Civil Rights Movement 1954-1985. "Freedom Songs." Arlington: Blackside PBS. 2009

Haddad, Lulie. Narrated by Louise Toussaint. "This Far by Faith, Part 3." Arlington: Blackside, Inc. & the Faith Project, Inc, PBS 2007.

"Say Amen, Somebody," sound recording: original soundtrack recording and more / a George T. Nierenberg film; album produced and mixed by Fordin, Hugh. New York: DRG Records, 1983.

Index

Abbington, James, 154–155
Academy of Gospel Music Arts, 104
Adams, Charles, 167
African Methodist Episcopal (AME) Church, 19–20, 35
African religious traditions, 15–17
"Alas and Did My Savior Bleed", 9
"All I Need Is Jesus", 70
Allen, Ernest, 139, 141
Allen, Lorraine, 139–142
Allen, Richard, 19–20
Allen, William Francis, 17
Anderson, Marian, 23
Anglican Church, 8–9, 15, 17, 19–20
Armstrong, Louis, 72
Armstrong, Vanessa Bell, 192
Asaph, 6–7
awards organizations, 103–106

Banfield, William C., 10
Banks, Lacy J., 82
barrelhouse blues, 32
Barrett Sisters, 143, 144
Barrett-Campbell, Delois, 142–144
Bay Psalm Book, The, 21
Beecher, Henry Ward, 26
Bentley, Carl, 136, 144–147
Berkeley, Shirley, 129
Bethel A.M.E. Church, 19–20
Biblical basis for music ministry, 5, 6, 176
black folk music, cultural influence of, 31–34
black historical experience, cultural reflection of, 32–34
"The Blood Will Never Lose Its Power," 92
blues
    black folk music, influence of, 32
    gospel music, resemblance to, 4, 14